ESSENTIALS of Sarbanes-Oxley

Essentials Series

The Essentials Series was created for busy business advisory and corporate professionals. The books in this series were designed so that these busy professionals can quickly acquire knowledge and skills in core business areas.

Each book provides need-to-have fundamentals for those professionals who must:

- Get up to speed quickly, because they have been promoted to a new position or have broadened their responsibility scope
- Manage a new functional area
- Brush up on new developments in their area of responsibility
- Add more value to their company or clients

Other books in this series include:

Essentials of Accounts Payable, Mary S. Schaeffer
Essentials of Balanced Scorecard, Mohan Nair
Essentials of Capacity Management, Reginald Tomas Yu-Lee
Essentials of Capital Budgeting, James Sagner
Essentials of Cash Flow, H.A. Schaeffer, Jr.
Essentials of Corporate Performance Measurement, George T. Friedlob, Lydia L.F. Schleifer, and Franklin J. Plewa, Jr.
Essentials of Cost Management, Joe and Catherine Stenzel
Essentials of Credit, Collections, and Accounts Receivable, Mary S. Schaeffer
Essentials of CRM: A Guide to Customer Relationship Management, Bryan Bergeron
Essentials of Financial Analysis, George T. Friedlob and Lydia L. F. Schleifer
Essentials of Financial Risk Management, Karen A. Horcher
Essentials of Intellectual Property, Paul J. Lerner and Alexander I. Poltorak
Essentials of Knowledge Management, Bryan Bergeron
Essentials of Patents, Andy Gibbs and Bob DeMatteis
Essentials of Payroll Management and Accounting, Steven M. Bragg
Essentials of Shared Services, Bryan Bergeron
Essentials of Supply Chain Management, Michael Hugos
Essentials of Trademarks and Unfair Competition, Dana Shilling
Essentials of Treasury, Karen A. Horcher
Essentials of Managing Corporate Cash, Michele Allman-Ward and James Sagner
Essentials of XBRL, Bryan Bergeron

For more information on any of the above titles, please visit www.wiley.com

ESSENTIALS
of Sarbanes-Oxley

Sanjay Anand

John Wiley & Sons, Inc.

This book is printed on acid-free paper. ♾

Published by John Wiley & Sons, Inc., Hoboken, New Jersey.

Wiley Bicentennial Logo: Richard J. Pacifico.

Published simultaneously in Canada.

For general information on our other products and services, or technical support, please contact our Customer Care Department within the United States at 800-762-2974, outside the United States at 317-572-3993, or fax 317-572-4002.

Wiley also publishes its books in a variety of electronic formats. Some content that appears in print may not be available in electronic books.

For more information about Wiley products, visit our Web site at http://www.wiley.com.

Library of Congress Cataloging-in-Publication Data

Anand, Sanjay.
Essentials of Sarbanes-Oxley / Sanjay Anand.
p. cm.
Includes index.

ISBN 978-0-470-05668-4 (pbk.)

1. United States. Sarbanes-Oxley Act of 2002. 2. Corporations–Accounting–Law and legislation–United States. 3. Disclosure of information–Law and legislation–United States. 4. Financial statements–Law and legislation–United States. 5. Directors of corporations–Legal status, laws, etc.–United States. 6. Corporate governance–Law and legislation–United States. I. Title.

KF1446.A315A83 2007

346.73'0666–dc22

Printed in the United States of America

10 9 8 7 6 5 4 3 2 1

To my parents

Contents

Foreword

In the past decade I, like so many others, observed carefully as the ethical fabric of corporate America fell to shreds. I watched CEO after CEO paraded in front of the public for their crimes. But I saw more than what the news cameras showed; I saw the danger of history repeating itself.

Fraud hurts business. When it occurs on as grand a scale as we witnessed, it hurts the economy as a whole. I anticipated and hoped that some measures would be taken to reinstate public trust in our markets.

When the Sarbanes-Oxley Act (SOX) was first introduced, I heard the collective gasp rise up from Corporate America. We all knew that this Act was not going to make life easy for corporations, but there was hope that the efforts would be worthwhile.

As someone who has dedicated his professional career to fraud prevention and education, I felt motivated and inspired. I knew that with education and assistance, companies could achieve compliance. In SOX I saw a chance to reinstate American corporations as pinnacles of business, fit for emulation.

The first years were as rough as I predicted they would be; costs were high and knowledge was low, which can be a disheartening situation. I believed that with the right guidance, companies could work within the SOX framework and build a balance between their needs and those of their shareholders.

We have seen this to be true. The costs of compliance are becoming increasingly more manageable as information and education have improved. I anticipate seeing even greater improvements in the years to come, and this book is going to have a hand in creating those improvements.

I have been privileged to work with Sanjay through the SOX Institute. He subscribes to the same belief that I do: Educating people makes the difference. Companies will have greater compliance success when they have a strong team holding them up.

Sanjay believes, and teaches, that when a company has the knowledge, the ethics, and the leadership, it will achieve compliance.

I am thrilled that Sanjay has chosen to complement his growing library and write a book that reaches out to the expanding audience of those impacted by SOX. His sharing of his knowledge of governance, his experience with companies and corporations around the globe, and his expertise with the Act is truly valuable.

As a strategic advisor and certified consultant, Sanjay has worked with the roll call of Fortune 500 and Global 2000 companies. These companies have benefited not only from his intelligence and knowledge, but also from his innovation and dedication. I know that they join my commendation of this book.

I have heard Sanjay referred to as the "consultant's consultant." Every time he sees a gap in knowledge and understanding, he works tirelessly to fill it. He sees the changing environment of SOX as an endless source of opportunities to educate.

This book does just that. It fills the gaps and ensures that everyone impacted by SOX will have the information at his or her fingertips. Better yet, it explains the concepts in a straightforward manner that is so refreshing in our world of jargon.

This is the book that should be on the CEO's nightstand, in the board member's gym bag, and the MBA student's hand. It fills the gaps between theory and execution, and teaches us all those important lessons of compliance.

No professional should be without a copy of this book.

Professor Tommy Seah
CFE, CMC, FAIA, ACIB, MIIA, FIFA, AICFA, CSOXP
Vice-Chairman, Board of Regents
Association for Certified Fraud Examiners (ACFE)

Preface

In 2002 the U.S. Senate added the Sarbanes-Oxley Act (SOX) to the network of securities regulations that it has been building to keep corporate America in check. This Act was fledged from a desire to protect investors, and the U.S. economy, from the threat of scandal and corruption in publicly traded companies. In an effort to ward off future Kenneth Lays and Arthur Andersens, SOX establishes strict expectations and imposes even stricter penalties for compliance failure.

Some would argue that the penalty of such rash legislation may be too high of a price for innocent companies to shoulder as punishment for sharing the title of "publicly traded" with a few bad apples.

Irrespective of whether SOX and its regulations are necessary or even desirable, they are a fact of life for publicly traded businesses in the U.S. markets. SOX is a reality that needs to be understood, accommodated, and, when possible, mastered in order for companies to balance their compliance efforts with their business interests

Who This Book Is For

This book is for the senior-level professionals, the executives, and the board members whose companies are impacted by SOX. It is for those who are looking for the knowledge to initiate a SOX project or allocate a budget.

This book is also for any professional or consultant who would like to be able to discuss SOX in an intelligent and informed manner.

SOX affects all company members, from the CEO to middle management and beyond. Compliance is a collective effort, and by understanding the Act, you will be able to question, discuss, and contribute.

How to Use This Book

In these pages you will find information that will help you to understand SOX and the implications that it has for your company, plus specific explanations on how to help your company achieve compliance.

In addition, this book has been designed with appreciation and respect for your demanding lifestyle and professional obligations. With a clear overview, as well as chapter summaries at both the start and end of chapters, this book ensures that information is easy to find and always at your fingertips.

Although the book is arranged in the manner that seemed to flow most logically, there is no need to read the chapters in their presented order. Feel confident to skip around, knowing that each chapter can be read as a stand-alone article, designed to present you with complete information.

What You Will Find

A brief summary of each of the chapters in this book follows. These summaries will help you to better understand why each topic was chosen and also assist you to find specific information that you are looking for.

- Chapter 1 begins our tour of SOX with a history lesson. It explains the events that led to the inception of the Act, as well as the two men who were so instrumental in its development, Congressman Oxley and Senator Sarbanes.

  It is important to understand the circumstances surrounding the development of SOX in order to truly understand why it was developed and what it seeks to achieve. Essentially this Act is meant to reinstate the trust that investors, employees, and the general public once had for publicly traded companies. This trust is a vital part of our economy, and maintaining it is a worthwhile goal.

  This chapter provides readers with a background of the Act that will serve as a springboard for the rest of the knowledge that they gain throughout the book. Only by understanding where it came from can we truly understand where SOX is today and where it is headed in the future.

- In Chapter 2 the issues of SOX are examined and the Act's core concepts are discussed. This chapter walks through the key principles of the Act as well as those issues that are related to its compliance. Before taking a more in-depth look at how compliance can be achieved and the tools that are required for such an endeavor, it is important that the foundations of the Act are understood.

  By taking a bird's eye view of the Act and discussing some of the big issues, this chapter provides readers with a structured framework on which to build their SOX knowledge. The key to understanding SOX, legislation that was designed with a very specific purpose in mind, is found in understanding the big issues with which it deals.

- Chapter 3 provides an overview of some of the most applicable SOX sections. This chapter not only explains what the Act actually says, it also explains the consequences of the requirements and illustrates some challenges that companies may face in their compliance efforts.

  While reading this chapter, it is important to keep in mind that although some sections of SOX receive more attention than others, the Act itself is meant to be treated as a whole. Unlike other pieces of legislation in which some sections apply to certain segments, SOX, for the most part, is applicable in its entirety.

  By highlighting some of the most important sections of the Act, this chapter gives an overview of compliance efforts and provides a picture of what SOX, as a whole, is working to achieve.

- Chapter 4 offers practical information that has been designed to facilitate an understanding of SOX through the compliance process. Reading this chapter will not only provide a general framework for the compliance strategy; it will also illustrate the challenges that many companies face in meeting the SOX regulations.

  Although each company will have its own unique strategy for compliance that will reflect the circumstances in which it finds itself, there is a general process that all SOX efforts follow.

Reading through the common steps taken for compliance will solidify the ideas learned in earlier chapters and provide concrete implications for SOX's general principles and specific sections.

- No book related to SOX is complete without a discussion of the Committee of Sponsoring Organizations (COSO) and the Control Objectives for Information and Related Technology (COBIT). These two frameworks will be covered in Chapter 5. This chapter provides readers with information about these specific frameworks and further explains compliance efforts and the many forms that they can take.

  Although the Securities and Exchange Commission (SEC), Public Company Accounting Oversight Board (PCAOB), and SOX do not provide very much guidance as to how to achieve compliance, the SEC has specifically recommended that management use COSO or a framework that is very similar. Almost all companies follow that recommendation.

  As the templates used to evaluate the efficacy of all other frameworks, COSO, COBIT, and the information provided in this chapter are all vital components of SOX compliance.

- Chapter 6 takes ones of the largest issues dealing with compliance and breaks it down to explain why the cost of SOX compliance is a major concern and how that concern is manageable with the right strategies. Many of the factors that have contributed to high compliance costs in previous years are being mitigated by the development of new technology and more efficient systems. This chapter provides insight into the ways that technology contributes to sustainable compliance.

SOX compliance would be easily achieved with a limitless budget, but this is not reality. Companies do require cost controls in order to ensure that their compliance strategies are sustainable and that they fit within the parameters of maintaining a healthy bottom line.

- Chapter 7 focuses on information technology (IT). Although IT is not specifically mentioned in the Act, its involvement is implicit, given the technological nature of our times. This chapter is designed to provide readers with an overview of the role that IT and IT divisions play in SOX compliance efforts. Internal controls over financial processes are integrally linked to the IT systems that the company has established. IT is also instrumental in the establishment of controls and their testing processes, which actually helps to keep such tasks manageable and efficient.

  After reading this chapter, readers should have an overall impression of what IT's role is in compliance and an idea of the steps that an IT division should take to facilitate its company's SOX efforts.

- Although publicly traded companies are the ones most obviously targeted by SOX, several other organizations are impacted by the Act as well. Chapter 8 explores the ways in which entities outside of Corporate America are dealing with SOX and what specific challenges they face. The four major groups that are impacted by SOX compliance are those that provide outsourcing services, the publicly traded companies, foreign issuers, and not-for-profit organizations.

This chapter takes the information learned throughout the book and extrapolates it to involve some of the issues just outside the realm of general SOX conversation. These issues provide readers with a chance to understand and become aware of the wide-reaching scope of this legislation.

My Goal for You

My goal in writing this book was to remove SOX from the philosophical and theoretical realm and bring it into the real world, which is where it is having its effect. It is time that SOX compliance was discussed in terms of action rather than ideals because it is the actions that create the compliance.

I hope that this book provides you with the knowledge and information to feel confident with the concept of SOX and the impact that it is having on the face of business.

Regardless of where SOX takes us from here or where we were before its inception, what matters is that it is impacting the face of business today. This book is designed to help those affected by SOX to understand their compliance efforts and make the most of the process.

Acknowledgments

My sincerest thanks to . . . (in alphabetical order by last name to be fair)

Shannon Brayford for patiently editing and reediting and re-reediting and . . . (you get the idea)

Sheck Cho, Executive Editor, and others on his team at John Wiley & Sons, Inc., for their guidance

Debi Deimling at Congressman Oxley's office for her encouragement (she calls me "Mr. SOX")

Congressman Michael Oxley, Honorary Chairperson, SOX Institute, for his encouragement

Dennis O'Connor of Paradigm Communications for helping to promote this book

Robert Schwind for his valuable inputs and insights to make sure I was "on track"

Tommy Seah, Certified Fraud Examiner in Practice, for agreeing to write the foreword for this book

Ethiopis Tafara, Director, Office of International Affairs, SEC for his article in Chapter 8.

CHAPTER 1

Background

After reading this chapter, you will be able to:

- Understand the historical environment from which the Sarbanes-Oxley Act (SOX) was born.
- Understand the key principles in the development of the Act.
- Understand the role of the Securities and Exchange Commission (SEC) and Public Company Accounting Oversight Board (PCAOB) in SOX-related regulation development and enforcement.

Introduction

The Sarbanes-Oxley Act (Publication License No. 107-204, 116 Stat. 745) is a U.S. federal law that is known by several names, including:

- Public Company Accounting Reform and Investor Protection Act of 2002
- SOA
- SOX
- SarbOx

This law was created, in part, as a reaction to the corporate corruption scandals that occurred during the late 1990s and early 2000s. One of the primary objectives of the Act was to establish clear accounting and reporting practices for both the boards of publicly traded U.S. companies and public accounting firms. This was done in the hope of reinstating the trust of investors and the general public.

Essentially, SOX requires that every publicly traded company's executive members evaluate and hold responsibility for the accuracy and completeness of all financial information that is released. This Act also requires that companies release information regarding those controls that are in place to ensure the accuracy of the financial information.

This chapter introduces the history of SOX and provides insight into the circumstances that resulted in its enactment.

Corporate Scandals

In the years surrounding the turn of the twenty-first century, several high-profile corporate scandals shook public trust. Insider trading, fraudulent financial records, and other deceitful incidents caused investors to question the integrity of the stock markets and their listed companies.

The poster children of this era include WorldCom, Enron, and Tyco International.[1] The exploits of some of their key executives resulted in document manipulation to facilitate insider trades, hide debts, and inflate assets, in an effort to purposely mislead investors.

- *WorldCom.* As chief executive officer (CEO) of WorldCom, Bernard Ebbers was able to amass a large fortune during the 1990s. Ebbers used his stock holdings to finance personal ventures and further increase his assets. In the year 2000 WorldCom's stock began its decline, and Ebbers was unable to cover his stock's margin calls. To raise the funds Ebbers turned to WorldCom's board of directors for loans and guarantees worth over $400 million.

  Ebbers resigned from his position in mid-2002 after a federal probe began in April of that year into both his loans and WorldCom's accounting practices. That June the SEC filed fraud charges against WorldCom, and on March 15, 2005, Ebbers was convicted on charges of fraud and conspiracy.

  His legal conviction carried a sentence of 25 years in prison, which Ebbers is currently serving in a Louisiana federal prison. The former CEO has also agreed to civil lawsuit settlements that require the relinquishment of his assets.

  Additionally, civil settlements also require Ebbers to issue financial restitution of $6 billion the investors that he defrauded.

Although significant, this is relatively inconsequential when compared to the $180 billion lost by investors as a direct result of the WorldCom fraud.

- *Enron scandal.* As the United States' seventh largest company, Enron once employed more than 21,000 people in over 40 countries. During its time on top, Enron was a major corporate competitor and held close ties with the White House.

  In September 2006, Enron sold its last remaining business, Prisma International, thus completing its transition from industry leader to assetless corporation.

  The company experienced its collapse as a direct result of corporate accounting fraud. In order to mislead investors and maintain its successful image, Enron manipulated its financial appearance by lying about profits and hiding debts.

  Several Enron executives were convicted on charges related to fraud and conspiracy. For example, Andrew Fastow, chief financial officer (CFO), was sentenced to 10 years in prison and ordered to forfeit $24 million. Kenneth Lay, CEO, was also convicted and faced 45 years in prison after his conviction, but died before the sentence was handed down.

- *Tyco International scandal.* Tyco International's CEO, Dennis Kozlowski, and CFO, Mark Swartz, were convicted on June 17, 2005, of stealing $600 million from the corporation. Their actions not only defrauded investors, but also directly resulted in the loss of several thousand jobs.

  Unlike Enron and WorldCom, Tyco International has been able to persevere through the scandal. Although suffering severe financial setbacks, the company has rearranged assets, sold smaller businesses, and worked to regain the trust of investors.

Unfortunately, these are not the only scandals that scar corporate America's past, although they are the ones that have received the most attention. These events created a collective sense of dishonesty and disregard for the rights of investors that has led to a breakdown of the trust that the public had for the U.S. markets and their company members.

Investor, Employee, and Public Trust

News of corporate corruption works to erode the trust of investors and employees whose resources are vital components of a company's success. When a specific act of fraud or corruption occurs, the company feels the direct impact. However, corruption also creates a trickle-down effect whereby all companies in the economy suffer.

Investor trust in publicly traded companies is integral to the success of the trading system. Profiles of incidences of corporate scandal and investor deception serve to create investors' suspicion in all companies in which they invest. The collective result is that reasonable traders start to question whether their investments are being respected and whether they are being treated fairly. Essentially, shareholders can be abused only so many times before they start to become wary.

With enough occurrences of fraud, investors begin to invest more conservatively in order to protect their finances. Without investor activity, the U.S. stock markets would collapse and publicly traded companies would suffer. The result would be severe economic recession as seen in the Great Depression following the stock market crash of 1929.

IN THE REAL WORLD

Stock Exchange Crash in October 1929

We are all aware of the economic ramifications that the stock market crash of 1929 had on the United States and countries whose economy is directly linked to that of the United States.

After the reign of a bull market, the stocks of the New York Stock Exchange lost over 83% of their value between September 1929 and July 1932. This staggering collapse created unthinkable ramifications both nationally and abroad. Through this crash banks lost money, companies lost their fortunes, and the public lost not only their savings and jobs, but also their faith in the market. The result was the Great Depression, which plagued the economy for many years.

After the crash, members of the U.S. government agreed that part of their concerted effort to restore the health of the economy had to focus on reinstating people's trust in the capital markets. They knew that unless citizens felt comfortable investing in the future of their country's companies, industries, and markets would not recover.

This led to the creation of the Securities Act of 1933, which demanded that all publicly traded companies release their financial information to the public. Had such practices been established earlier, it is possible that the Great Depression would never have occurred.

The goal of the Securities Act was to make the investing process more transparent and eliminate the practice of insider trading. The overall objective was to provide investors with assurance that history would not repeat itself and that the stock market would be a safe place to invest.

In The Real World (continued)

As a vehicle for enforcing the Securities Act, the U.S. government also passed the Securities Exchange Act of 1934. This Act created the SEC and outlined the commission's powers and goals.

The Securities Acts of the 1930s were effective in reassuring investors of the market's safety, and the SEC is still a viable power within the corporate world. Yet since the 1930s, the landscape of corporate America has undergone major changes. Although still applicable and relevant, these earlier acts have lost some of their previous control.

Over the course of 70 years, the nature of business, the global markets, and the sophistication of legal and accounting systems have created gaps in the controls of the securities laws. Even though the SEC sought to retain control through new regulations and amendments, the corporate scandals of the last decade demonstrated that new legislation was long past due.

In a sense, SOX seeks to reestablish the goals of the Securities Acts and make them applicable and relevant to the corporate world in the twenty-first century. This Act is designed to cover new circumstances that were not an issue during the 1930s, such as Internet, email, privacy regulations, and the ubiquitous global market.

Proponents of this Act hope that it also will reestablish investor trust in the market and enforce a corporate culture of ethical behavior and respect for shareholders. Although another depression may not be on the horizon, it is clear that fostering confidence in publicly traded companies will serve a greater economic good.

In addition to investor trust, it is also important to consider the implications that a lack of trust can have on employees. Although stock market and financial activity are not the only factors that contribute to an employee's impression of corporate management and executive boards, deceitful or fraudulent behaviors do have the potential for creating a contributing effect. There is a risk that employees working in the nonexecutive levels of corporations will assume that those running all companies are untrustworthy. Not only can this compromise the company's productivity, it also can create a culture of dishonesty in which lower-level frauds may also occur.

When a company suffers in the aftermath of a scandal, employees face the financial consequences of job loss and cutbacks. In times when scandals appear to abound, employees may experience fear of job insecurity, even if their executive members hold high ethical standards.

The aftermath of scandals such as Enron, WorldCom, and Tyco International has demonstrated these effects, but companies are making efforts to rectify the problem. The Watson Wyatt Work USA Survey (2004)[2] reported that just over 51% of respondents felt that their senior management was trustworthy.

IN THE REAL WORLD

Securities Act of 1933 and Securities Exchange Act of 1934

Following the collapse of the New York Stock Exchange in 1929, Congress passed the Securities Act of 1933 and the Securities Exchange Act of 1934. The Securities Act of 1933 seeks to ensure that investors receive truthful and representative information about publicly traded companies; the Securities Exchange Act of 1934 created the SEC and provided it with powers over the securities industry to facilitate the fair treatment of investors.

Corporate Governance

At the heart of corporate governance is the ideal that a company's financial and business goals can be balanced with social and ethical considerations. In fact, many believe that a company's financial and business goals can actually be served by conscious policies toward ethical behavior.

Although corporate governance is not a new concept, it is an ever-evolving one. As different models demonstrate success, the world's opinion of the best standard changes and new corporate governance standards gain favor.

During the rampage of corporate scandal, the U.S. model fell temporarily out of favor. Nevertheless, as the economy and corporate culture regain their footing, U.S. corporate governance standards are reestablishing themselves in the eyes of the world.

History of the Sarbanes-Oxley Act

The history of SOX centers on two elected officials, Senator Paul Sarbanes (D-Md) and Congressman Michael Oxley (R-Oh). As the corporate scandals of the late 1990s reached their pinnacle, the U.S. Government recognized that they would have to make a concerted effort to prove to investors that their interests were important.

In April 2002 Congressman Oxley put forth the Corporate and Auditing Accountability, Responsibility, and Transparency Act (CAARTA).[3] This bill sought to reinforce the ideals of the Securities Laws of the 1930s and eliminate the perception that corporations were blameless entities. CAARTA was passed on April 25, 2005, by the

House of Representatives with a vote of 334 to 90. Congressman Oxley's bill then proceeded to the Senate Banking Committee for further approval.

Around the same time, Senator Sarbanes, head of the Senate Banking Committee, was preparing a similar proposal. His bill, Senate Bill 2673,[4] also sought to bring the ideals of integrity and accountability back to the corporate world. Bill 2673 passed the Senate Banking Committee on June 18, 2002, by a vote of 17 to 4. The bill then moved to the U.S. Senate, where it received unanimous support of voting members with a vote of 97 to 0, on July 15, 2002.

In order to reconcile both Congressman Oxley's CAARTA and Senator Sarbanes' SB 2673, the House of Representatives and the Senate formed a Conference Committee. The resultant bill was the Public Company Accounting Reform and Investor Protection Act. This bill, which later became commonly known as the Sarbanes-Oxley Act, was approved by the House with a vote of 423 to 3 and by the Senate with a vote of 99 to 0.

Senator Paul Sarbanes

A Rhodes Scholar and lawyer by trade, Senator Paul Sarbanes introduced the first Article of Impeachment against President Richard Nixon while holding office in the House of Representatives.[5]

During his fourth term in the U.S. Senate, Senator Sarbanes served as the chairman of the Senate Banking, House, and Urban Affairs Committee. It was in this role that he held a series of hearings regarding the Enron scandal and established the bill that led to the Sarbanes-Oxley Act.

IN THE REAL WORLD

Senate Banking, House, and Urban Affairs Committee

This U.S. Senate Committee oversees matters related to banks, price controls, export controls, federal monetary policy, currency and coinage, public and private housing, urban development, and mass transit. It is chaired by a senator of the majority party and is responsible for reviewing, editing, and passing all bills relevant to matters under their control.

Congressman Michael Oxley

Born February 11, 1944, Congressman Michael Oxley practiced law before being elected to the Congress. As a member of the House of Representatives, Congressman Oxley served 12 terms. This fiscal conservative has worked throughout his career to promote economic, technological, and telecommunications advancements.[6]

SEC and PCAOB

Publicly traded companies have always been very familiar with the Securities and Exchange Commission through both its requirements and a variety of quarterly and annual forms. Now these companies have a second organization with which to interact. SOX Section 101 created the Public Company Accounting Oversight Board and assigned its powers and jurisdictions.

Although both organizations are concerned with maintaining the integrity of the U.S. public market system, the SEC and PCAOB rule over different areas of the process. It is also important to understand that while the SEC is a government-appointed commission, the PCAOB is a private not-for-profit organization. This distinction does have an impact on how these two organizations are received by the corporate world.

SEC

After the New York Stock Exchange crash in 1929, the U.S. Congress determined that significant changes to the market's operations would have to be established in order to restore the public's faith in capital markets. Because of these efforts, the Congress enacted the Securities Act of 1933 and the Securities Exchange Act of 1934. The first of these acts set forth the mandates for companies to follow, and the second established the SEC to govern over compliance.

The SEC's role is to enforce the Securities Act of 1933 and therefore protect investors. The primary objective of this Commission is to defend the concept that all investors, regardless of whether they are a large institution or a private individual, have a right to sound facts about their investments. To this end, the SEC requires public companies to disclose their financial and other relevant information to the public. Ideally, this should make for efficient information flow and a more transparent market.

In more recent years, the SEC's ability to govern publicly traded companies and their activities has fallen under criticism. It was because of the Commission's failure to effectively prevent the corporate scandals of the last decade that the U.S. government sought to increase investor security through SOX.

IN THE REAL WORLD

SEC Investigations

The SEC has jurisdiction to investigate those companies it suspects are involved in unethical or illegal trade activities. The Commission maintains information on companies through mandatory submissions of quarterly and annual reports, and uses these reports as the basis of its investigations.

The SEC pursues an investigation if it suspects that members of a company are involved in any of these activities:

- Insider trading
- Information misrepresentation
- Stock price manipulation
- Fund or securities theft
- Unregistered securities sales

SEC Internal Organization

The SEC is a federal agency of over 3,000 staff organized into 18 offices and 4 divisions. Leading the operations are five presidentially appointed commissioners, one of whom is the chairperson. One of the four, the Division of Corporate Finance, oversees publicly traded companies and their disclosure of important information in compliance with the Securities Act of 1933. Additional activities of this division include serving as a liaison between companies and the Securities Act. In this capacity, the division is responsible for providing instructions and assistance to facilitate companies' efforts at complying with SEC rules and regulations.

IN THE REAL WORLD

No-Action Letters

In one of its many roles, the SEC's Division of Corporation Finances serves as a liaison between publicly traded companies and the SEC. One of the most important functions that this division provides in this capacity is the issuance of no-action letters.

Companies will request a no-action letter when they are about to embark into uncharted activities that may or may not result in SEC investigation. To obtain guidance as to whether their actions will result in unpleasant consequences, companies submit an outline of their intended activities. After reviewing those activities, the Division of Corporation Finances releases a judgment as to whether it would or would not recommend SEC action against a company that acted in this manner.

Essentially these letters serve as a hypothetical "if I did this ... would you?" interaction between the SEC and the company.

TIPS AND TECHNIQUES

Documents Reviewed by the SEC Division of Corporation Finance

Depending on the nature of a public company and its financial organization, the SEC requires the submission of several reports and statements each year. The relevant division reviews these statements. The Division of Corporation Finance is responsible for:

- New securities registration statements
- Forms 10-K and 10-Q

Tips and Techniques (continued)

- Shareholder meeting material
- Documents of tender offers
- Merger and acquisition filings

PCAOB

The PCAOB was created by SOX to function as a private, nonprofit corporation reporting to the SEC. This organization oversees the auditors of public companies and their activities. In general, the purpose of the PCAOB is to protect investors and the public by ensuring informative and independent audit reports. It is through SOX Section 101 that the PCAOB has been ascribed its powers, which include:

- *Registering public accounting firms.* In an effort to uphold and regulate public accounting firms, the PCAOB has been instructed by SOX Section 101 to establish and maintain a registration of all those accounting firms that have publicly traded clients.
- *Setting standards for auditing, quality control, and ethics relating to issuer audit reports.* The scandals of the 1990s demonstrated that accountants can have a severe impact on corrupt practices either by direct and purposeful action or by failure to recognize the activities. By establishing the PCAOB as a regulatory board, SOX seeks to guide accounting firms in maintaining the highest level of standards and therefore preventing investor deception.

- *Inspect registered public accounting firms.* In addition to providing regulations for public accounting firms, the PCAOB has also been charged with the responsibility of inspecting those firms to ensure that compliance is maintained.
- *Lead investigations and disciplinary proceedings.* SOX provides the PCAOB with the power to investigate and charge accounting firms and associated persons when they fail to comply with standards set. The PCAOB is also able to impose sanctions, which include fines of up to $100,000 for individuals and $2 million for audit firms.

PCAOB Internal Organization

The board of the PCAOB includes five full-time members, including one chairperson. These members are appointed by the SEC through consultation with the chairperson of the Board of Governors of the Federal Reserve System and the Secretary of the Treasury. The rules stipulate that at least two of the five members must currently be, or have been in the past, certified public accountants (CPAs). The first appointed chairperson of the PCAOB was William J. McDonough, who served from May 21, 2003, until November 30, 2005, when he was succeeded by Mark W. Olson.

Unlike the SEC, board members of the PCAOB are not presidentially appointed. This fact has created a great deal of contention among those who disagree with SOX, especially because it does grant the PCAOB legal powers.

IN THE REAL WORLD

Lawsuit Challenging the Constitutionality of the PCAOB

On February 7, 2003, the Free Enterprise Fund and the Competitive Enterprise Institute launched a lawsuit against the Public Company Accounting Oversight Board.[a] Through this lawsuit, these organizations argue that the PCAOB violates Article II, Section 2 of the United States Constitution, referred to as the Appointments Clause.

The lawsuit asserts that in creating the PCAOB and assigning it regulatory powers, SOX has provided the organization with federal enforcement authority. The lawsuit further asserts that the PCAOB's powers violate the Appointments Clause because the members of the PCAOB are neither appointed by nor accountable to any political officers.

Although this lawsuit threatened to undo the PCAOB and therefore SOX, the PCAOB still exists and the lawsuit was ineffective.

[a] More information regarding this lawsuit is available through www.feinstitute.org.

Relating the SEC to the PCAOB

Within SOX Sections 104 and 105, the SEC is given the jurisdiction to oversee the activities of the PCAOB. That jurisdiction is limited, however, and does not include the right to control the PCAOB's regular inspections nor its special investigations. As a result, the SEC is unable to pursue investigations against a company even if it believes that the PCAOB was wrong in neglecting to investigate it.

This limitation of power can mean that the PCAOB is effectively not regulated in some important instances.

Additionally, while the SEC does have the ability to amend PCAOB rules and review its regulations and standards, doing so is a rare occurrence. The framework and process for such interactions are time consuming and costly, and are therefore rarely pursued. This further contributes to the PCAOB's sense of autonomy.

Conclusion

SOX was created to combat the declining trust that investors and the public had in American markets and their listed companies. In the past decade, this culture of distrust manifested itself with the uncovering of several corporate scandals in which shareholders were deceived as to the financial state of the companies in which they had invested.

The history of SOX centers on the work of Senator Paul Sarbanes and Congressman Michael Oxley. These men, and their respective houses, worked together to formulate an act that would hold publicly traded companies to a higher standard and require more transparent financial reporting methods to ensure the safety of shareholders' money.

After developing the framework of SOX, the U.S. Government handed the legislation, and the power to regulate its enforcement, over to the newly created PCAOB. Under the guidance of the SEC, the PCAOB is responsible for filling in the details for compliance and ensuring that the objectives of SOX are met.

The first step toward understanding SOX is understanding the history behind it. Armed with this knowledge, SOX, its current state, and its possibilities for the future become much more transparent.

Summary

- The Sarbanes-Oxley Act is a federal law that is known by many names, most notably SOX.
- SOX was created as a reaction to corporate scandals of the 1990s, particularly those of Enron, Tyco International, and WorldCom.
- SOX resulted from the efforts of Congressman Michael Oxley and Senator Paul Sarbanes.
- Corporate corruption abuse of shareholders and their money can threaten the publicly traded market.

Notes

1. More information on the WorldCom, Tyco International, and Enron scandals can be found through the *Washington Post* archives at www.washingtonpost.com and through the SEC site at www.sec.gov.
2. The Watson Wyatt Work Survey, www.watsonwyatt.com/surveys.
3. Corporate and Auditing Accountability, Responsibility, and Transparency Act, www.biblioteca.jus.gov.ar/House-3763.pdf.
4. Bill 2673, http://thomas.loc.gov/cgi-bin/query/R?r107:FLD001:S56684.
5. www.sarbanes.senate.gov.
6. www.oxley.house.gov.

CHAPTER 2

Introduction to the Sarbanes-Oxley Act

After reading this chapter, you will be able to:

- Understand the key principles of the Sarbanes-Oxley Act (SOX).
- Understand the difference between principle-based and rule-based legislation, and the importance of each.
- Understand the general requirements of SOX compliance.
- Understand the benefits of complying with SOX regulations.
- Understand the consequences of not achieving SOX compliance.
- Understand the general corporate perceptions of SOX.

Introduction

With the background understanding established of where SOX came from and the circumstances that led to its inception, it is time to delve into the Act itself. This chapter explains the concepts involved in the Act, including its key principles and the issues surrounding compliance.

This chapter also discusses two important SOX-related organizations: the Securities and Exchange Commission (SEC) and the Public Company Accounting Oversight Board (PCAOB). These organizations play a vital role in the development and enforcement of SOX regulations and understanding their functions is integral to understanding the Act itself.

Key Principles of SOX

After investor trust was shaken by corporate scandals, it became clear that some key principles of behavior were missing from the governance strategies of at least a few publicly traded companies. An image of ethical behavior and respect for shareholder money is a vital component of U.S. markets; without it, investment could wane, and the economy would be significantly impacted.

SOX is designed to reassure shareholders that their investments are being protected from scandal and deception. To this end, the Act sets forth guidelines that compel companies to provide investors with all of the information that they require to make sound investing decisions.

The damaging effects of cheating investors in the past can be rectified in the minds of current investors only if companies portray a

EXHIBIT 2.1

To Help Reestablish Investor Trust, the Regulations of the Sarbanes-Oxley Act are Based on Three Principles: Integrity, Accuracy, and Accountability.

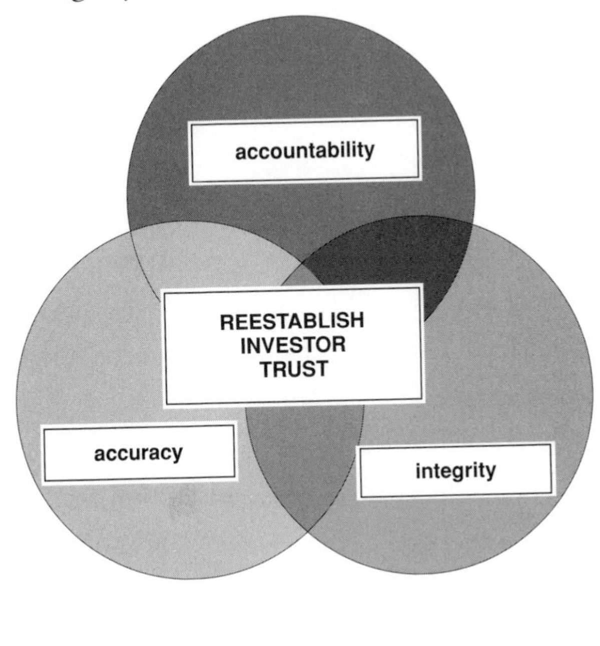

consistent and unified commitment to honesty and fairness. SOX was written in the spirit of three key principles: integrity, accuracy, and accountability (see Exhibit 2.1).

Integrity

The Act seeks to instill integrity into publicly traded companies. In order to maintain investor trust, it is vital that companies convey an image of high moral and professional standards. The goal of the Act is that, in time, investors will forgive past transgressions and recover their faith in the companies they invest in.

SOX also seeks to ensure the integrity of financial records in the sense that they are complete and representative. By requiring companies to present all relevant financial information, without exception, SOX hopes to eliminate fraudulent and erroneous reporting.

Accuracy

In addition to data integrity, SOX also seeks to ensure that the information that is reported is reliable and accurate. In the past, investors were without a clear benchmark standard or way of comparing security measures, as companies were left to determine their own security levels. By establishing a standard that is applied across the board, SOX seeks to create a system in which corrupt and misleading behaviors are prevented and detected. This provides investors with assurance that security measures are in place to protect the accuracy of the information that they receive, thereby protecting their investments.

Accountability

A common theme in past corporate scandals has been the elusive nature of the blamable party. It has seemed that within corporations, no members are culpable for the frauds, but rather the system creates an environment where blame can be passed and ignorance can be claimed.

SOX seeks to ensure that when fraudulent or misleading material is released to investors, there is a direct source for culpability and one or more parties will be held accountable. Through this Act, corporate executives and others responsible for financial reporting are answerable for breeches of information integrity and reliability. The motivation behind this principle is to eliminate the image of the "faceless corporation" and present both companies and the public with clear indications of which position is responsible for specific information and information-related tasks.

Principle- and Rule-Based Legislation

Looking back over history, there is a cyclical trend between principle- and rule-based legislations governing corporations and their accountants. For example, the generally accepted accounting principles[1] (GAAP) that emerged in the 1930s are the result of principle-based regulation. These principles reflect self-regulation, as GAAP was created by accountants, for accountants. The nature of such self-regulation is beneficial because it means that the principles are readily applicable and there is not the same growing pains seen when outsiders attempt to create rules for an industry.

Those who support principle-based legislation also argue that it provides freedom and flexibility for those applying it, while still enforcing codes to govern activities. Although this flexibility does provide benefits, such as the ability for the legislation to grow and advance with changes in the industry, it also has its drawbacks. For example, returning to GAAP, the self-regulation and flexibility found here has resulted in some negative effects regarding conflicts of interest. It is reasonable to suspect that an industry will not have a clear perspective on how best to regulate itself and that temptations or nearsightedness could lead to insufficiencies.

Those who feel that principle-based legislation has challenges would argue that accounting principles are not sufficient to prevent undesirable activities; for example, many of the actions taken during the Enron scandal were in fact consistent with GAAP.

Unlike principle-based legislation, rule-based legislation does not provide the same flexibility or self-regulation, meaning that it is more rigid and less vulnerable to conflicts of interest. However, rule-based legislation does have a steeper learning curve, and it can take longer before an industry is effectively able to adapt to the regulations.

For example, SOX has been designed to provide specific rules for auditors to directly prevent misrepresentation of financial information. The difficulty is that these rules have been laid out without instructions about how companies are to comply. It is from this lack of guidance that many SOX compliance issues have arisen.

Given the pros and cons of both principle- and rule-based legislation, there appears to be a solution: layering the two. By providing companies and auditors with the rules found in SOX, but supplying guidance through a series of principles such as GAAP and the Auditing Standards, a combination of rigid regulations and effective, flexible implementation can be achieved.

SOX Compliance

SOX mandates that its provisions be complied with by all companies in the United States that are publicly traded. Those companies that are initiating their initial public offering (IPO) also must comply with SOX. Additionally, SOX compliance is required of foreign companies under certain circumstances. One instance is in the case that a company exists outside of the United States but is a wholly owned subsidiary of a U.S. corporation. Non-U.S. companies that are publicly traded on U.S. markets through American Depository Receipts (ADRs) are also required to comply.

In the Real World

Who Else Is Affected?

SOX's primary objective is to protect those investors who purchase stocks on the U.S. markets, whether those investors are U.S. citizens or foreign purchasers. Although SOX primarily targets publicly traded companies that are listed on the U.S. markets, it also has significant implications that affect, both directly and indirectly, privately owned companies.

SOX contains provisions regarding document retention, criminal fraud, and Employee Retirement Income Security Act (ERISA); these issues are relevant to both privately and publicly owned companies. Moreover, any privately held company that seeks venture capital funding, commercial loans, or initial public offerings or that will conduct significant business with a publicly traded company is directly affected by SOX.

Although many will try to extrapolate SOX to make it applicable to private companies, that is not the intention of the Act. SOX was written to protect investors; however, regulations and provisions within the Act can be seen as a standard for financial reporting efforts in any company.

In cases where loan granters and other organizations require SOX compliance of private companies through their contracts, these requirements are not PCAOB related and are not enforceable by its standards.

General Compliance Requirements

To say that a company has achieved SOX compliance is largely to say that it has taken the necessary steps toward assuring the public of the accuracy of its financial reports. Such a distinction is meant to reassure investors that the information they receive from this company is valid and truthful.

In keeping with the three key principles of the Act—integrity, accuracy, and accountability—SOX compliance seeks to regulate

IN THE REAL WORLD

Asking Privately Held Companies to Achieve SOX Compliance

Although privately held companies are not legally compelled to comply with SOX standards, they are likely to feel market pressure to do so. SOX and its regulations are designed to benefit company shareholders by protecting their interests and ensuring that they receive complete and accurate information. In doing so, SOX allows shareholders to remain confident that they are basing their investment decisions on truthful information and they are not being deceived in any way.

It is reasonable to expect that industry regulators, lenders, insurers, government entities, and accountants who deal with private companies will encourage SOX-like compliance through their desire for similar benefits. Although such compliance efforts would not be enforceable through the PCAOB, no stipulation prevents financial institutions from requiring SOX compliance as a component of their contract requirements.

companies and their reporting activities. Compliance with SOX requires that the company release all relevant financial data to ensure the integrity of the information. It also requires that the data that is released is reliable to ensure its accuracy. Finally, it mandates that the chief executive officer (CEO) and chief financial officer (CFO) verify the data and accept accountability for any errors.

In order to ensure financial reporting practices are accurate, SOX requires that companies establish and maintain an accounting framework that includes internal controls. These controls are designed to secure the financial documents from error and misrepresentation, thereby protecting those who rely on the documents' accuracy. To this end, SOX compliance also requires that company executives assume responsibility for the establishment and maintenance of that framework.

Tips and Techniques

Steps Privately Held Companies Can Take toward Voluntary SOX Compliance

It is widely understood that SOX has been designed to protect the interests of the shareholders rather than those of the companies. The regulations and requirements of SOX compliance work to ensure that shareholders receive only accurate information and that their investments are not threatened by data errors or misrepresentations.

Tips and Techniques (continued)

Although not compelled to comply by the PCAOB or any other regulatory board, private companies may opt to achieve voluntary SOX compliance in order to offer their investors similar benefits and boost their image.

Privately held companies can take these steps toward achieving voluntary SOX compliance (see Exhibit 2.2).

Step 1. *Elect a board of independent members.* Even if it is just one, independent board members serve useful evaluation functions within a company and can function as the foundation for a future audit committee.

Step 2. *Create internal controls and perform baseline testing.* Doing so will enable the company to establish operational benchmarks and create an organizational framework for further compliance.

Step 3. *Adopt a formal code of business conduct and ethics.* Separate codes can be established for varying levels within the company that offer guidance specific to job descriptions.

Step 4. *Establish an internal audit function.* Whether through hiring a consultant or establishing a new position, the company can monitor and evaluate internal controls by establishing an internal audit function.

Step 5. *Require financial information certification.* Certifying financial information leads to enhancements in internal accounting competencies.

Step 6. *Control services that are provided by outside accounting firms and auditors.* By limiting the risk of external accountants providing conflicting services, companies will minimize problems with state regulators.

EXHIBIT 2.2

Nonprofit and Nonpublic Organizations May Choose to Initiate a Voluntary SOX Compliance Effort by the Steps Shown.

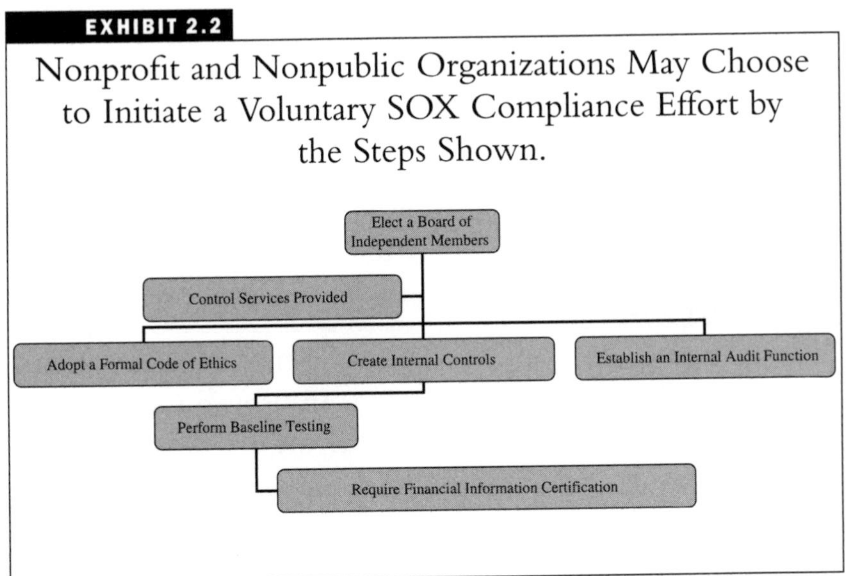

Benefits of Compliance

There are those companies that, regardless of whether they support SOX in general, have embraced the compliance efforts and even their associated costs as investments in their future. These companies view SOX regulations as standards that will improve their organization and facilitate their ability to control finances.

Some of the benefits of SOX compliance that can provide financial reward in the end include (see Exhibit 2.3):

- *Encouragement to organize and develop controls.* Many companies recognize the importance of establishing solid internal controls but find that doing so never seems to reach the top of their priority list. By mandating such actions, SOX forces companies to evaluate operations and establish a comprehensive framework of controls. As a result, the executive, board, audit committee, and management will be able to gain control over all aspects of operations, improving productivity and minimizing risks.

EXHIBIT 2.3

Although Compliance has Many Benefits, the Major Ones Include Fraud Prevention, Improved Company Image, Streamlined Year-End Process, Opportunity to Reevaluate and Improve Controls, and the Implementation of New Controls.

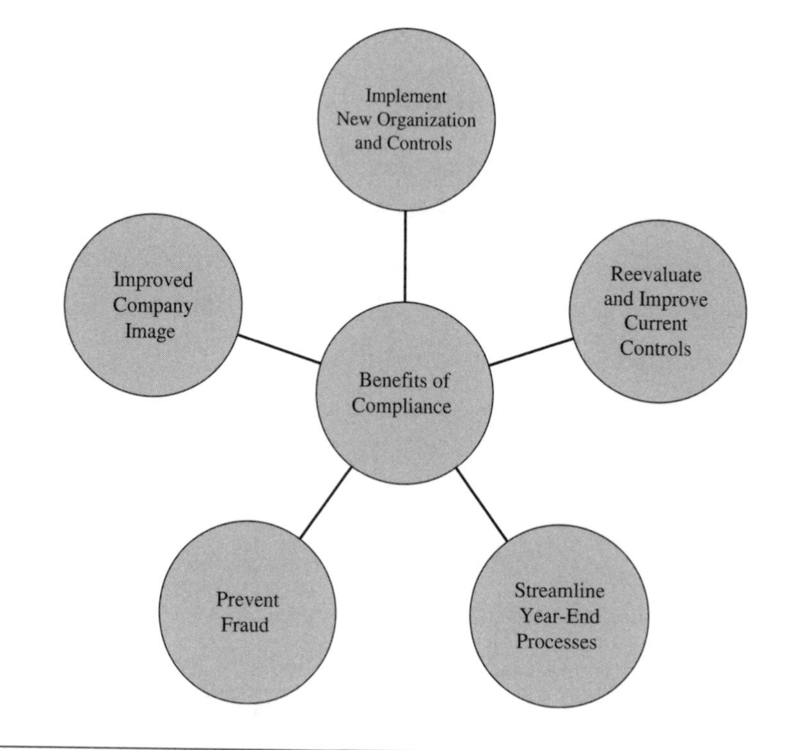

- *Encouragement to reevaluate and monitor current controls.* Through their efforts to comply with SOX, companies are forced to document and reevaluate already-established controls. Through this reevaluation, these companies can identify controls that have not been properly maintained and updated. By combining reevaluation of old controls with the redesign of new ones, companies are able to create a comprehensive system in a cost-efficient manner.
- *More organized year-end process.* Because SOX compliance forces companies to develop and integrate systems for document organization, it also keeps their financial records up-to-date and easily accessible. This additional attention and control in maintaining financial data and documents facilitates greater efficiency and better organization during the year-end process of SOX-compliant companies, thereby decreasing the costs and time associated with this process.
- *Prevention of fraud.* One of the greatest benefits of SOX is that it establishes requirements that are ultimately designed to protect from fraud. The increased security and antifraud protections required by SOX benefit companies by helping them to avoid the fates of Enron and other companies that suffered under scandal and went bankrupt.

Consequences of Noncompliance

Noncompliance with SOX falls directly on the shoulders of the executive officers who are required to certify the accuracy and integrity of the company's financial reports. In addition to civil lawsuits and damage to market image, CEOs and CFOs of companies that are noncompliant with SOX are subject to financial penalties and potential incarceration.

Situations where willful deceit cannot be proven carry fines of up to $1 million and 10 years in prison. However, in the event that wrongful certification has been submitted intentionally, the penalty maximum rises to $5 million and 20 years in prison.

Voluntary versus Mandatory Compliance

Since the passage of SOX, a great deal of philosophical and practical debate has been generated regarding whether corporate governance should be voluntary or mandatory. Those in favor of eliminating mandatory compliance and abolishing regulations such as SOX argue that companies have enough market incentive to adopt corporate governance policies voluntarily without the oversight of organizations such as the PCAOB.

Proponents of voluntary compliance argue against mandatory regulations, citing inefficiencies associated with broadly termed and widely scoped regulations. Pointing to high costs associated with SOX compliance, they argue that voluntary compliance would eliminate redundancy and allow companies to comply with only those regulations that directly apply to their operations. They also argue that organizations such as the PCAOB are unnecessary evils that create further financial burdens on companies through their fees, money that could be spent on greater controls.

Those in favor of mandatory compliance cite the fact that such regulations improve the public's ability to make informed decisions regarding investments, thereby improving market activities and generating further revenue for publicly traded companies. Supporters of SOX and similar regulations also cite historical cases of corruption as proof that voluntary compliance is ineffective. They argue that given the freedom to govern themselves, many companies will ignore the dangers associated with inadequate controls and will leave themselves and their investors open to deception in order to cut costs.

A third camp believes in the development of a compromise. Such a compromise could be a partially mandatory structure in which some SOX-like regulations would be enforced and others would be voluntary. One reconciliation that has been suggested is to propose recommendations, similar to those contained in SOX, for which compliance is voluntary, but mandate that companies disclose which recommendations they have complied with and how. This system of voluntary compliance and mandatory disclosure would provide investors with the information that they require and create greater market pressure toward compliance through competition over investment funds.

Irrespective of which camp is right and which is wrong, there is no indication that SOX will be going anywhere soon. It seems it is here to stay.

Corporate Perceptions of SOX

When SOX was passed, there was a consensus among the public, the government, and commercial leaders that some sort of action was required to prevent corporate scandals from continuing to erode the integrity of U.S. markets. Although there still appears to be a general consensus that action is required to rid the corporate landscape of corruption and reinstate public trust, there is a great deal of dissent regarding the specific actions taken by the government.

Several companies, accounting firms, and lobbyist groups have lodged various arguments against SOX and its enforcement. Two of the greatest complaints relate to the cost of compliance and the impact that the Act has on small businesses.

Although SOX is a controversial act that has created divided opinions regarding its necessity, fundamentals, and implementation, there are compliance benefits that improve the functioning of participating companies. Those organizations that choose to focus on these benefits will find that they have a much easier time accepting SOX and driving their compliance efforts forward.

Conclusion

SOX and everything related to its enactment is based on three core principles: integrity, accountability, and accuracy. Essentially, these are the three principles that appeared to be lacking in those companies that experienced corruption and fraud. It is important that shareholders and the general public are able to trust that financial records will be complete and provide true information. It is also important that if error or misrepresentation occurs, an established system is in place to hold culprits accountable.

Two types of regulations are applicable to corporations: principle- and rule-based legislation. Principle-based legislation offers flexibility and greater ease of application, while rule-based provides more rigid regulations and greater external control. Each has its pros and cons, and there is room for both within a greater framework of governance. For example, GAAP and SOX are able to work together for overall protection that is both feasible and enforceable.

The greatest action associated with SOX is the achievement of compliance. To comply with the Act means that the company has taken the necessary measures to pass its SOX audits and has been identified as a company that provides accurate financial information.

When a company achieves compliance, it not only provides its shareholders with greater security, it also provides itself with several financial rewards. These rewards include the benefits of greater system efficiency, less loss due to error, greater ease filing taxes, and less risk of fraud.

Summary

- The three core principles of SOX are accountability, accuracy, and integrity.
- SOX seeks to provide rule-based legislation to fill the gaps that principle-based regulation cannot fill.
- SOX compliance requires that the company take all necessary steps to ensure that its financial reports are accurate and complete.
- SOX mandates that CEOs and CFOs certify the accuracy of all financial reports and the efficacy of the controls that offer security to financial reporting systems.

Note

1. More information about GAAP can be found at www.fasab.gov/accepted.html.

CHAPTER 3

Selected SOX Sections

After reading this chapter, you will be able to:

- Understand the implications that Section 103 holds for auditors of publicly traded companies.
- Understand the provisions of Section 201 and the activities that it deems to be beyond the scope of an auditor.
- Understand Section 302, the importance of the June Proposals, and those Securities and Exchange Commission (SEC) forms that are impacted.
- Understand the compliance requirements of Section 404 and the steps that a company can take toward compliance.
- Understand the importance of a code of ethics and how this relates to Section 406.

- Understand the implications that Section 409 has for the filing of SEC Form 8-K.
- Understand whistle-blowers, their importance, and the protections offered by Section 806.

Introduction

The Sarbanes-Oxley Act (SOX) was not written to be considered in parts or to be complied with section by section. Instead, the Act was designed to serve as a comprehensive unit, and it was intended that the text be taken as a complete regulation.

All sections of SOX hold relevance for companies that are required to comply, and it is important that companies understand the importance of the Act in its entirety. That said, there are certain SOX sections that are more representative of the Act's intentions. There are also specific sections that received a great deal of attention either because of the direct impact on the compliance expectations or because of ambiguities and difficulties that they posed.

This chapter highlights some of the most frequently encountered sections of SOX and explains their relevance, as well as any important challenges associated with them. These highlighted sections include:

- Section 103: Auditing, Quality Control, and Independence Standards and Rules
- Section 201: Services Outside the Scope of Practice of Auditors
- Section 302: Corporate Responsibility for Financial Reports
- Section 404: Management Assessment of Internal Controls
- Section 406: Code of Ethics for Senior Financial Officers

TIPS AND TECHNIQUES

Regulations for Executive Directors and Officers

Although SOX places most of its weight on the shoulders of a company's CEO and CFO, some regulations also apply to executive directors and officers in general. One such regulation is the requirement that blackout periods be observed. These periods are time during which no stock associated with their employment or service can be bought or sold.

The goal of this regulation is to prevent the temptation for such company members to engage in insider trading; an activity that can severely compromise a company's stocks and shareholders.

- Section 409: Real-Time Issuer Disclosures
- Section 806: Protection for Employees of Publicly Traded Companies Who Provide Evidence of Fraud

Section 103: Auditing, Quality Control, and Independence Standards and Rules

SOX Section 103 is directly related to certified public accountants (CPAs) and the reports that they issue regarding public companies. CPAs are an integral part of the financial reporting practices of the companies that they serve. CPA firms not only provide financial services, but they also frequently function in a consulting and advising role, which serves to integrate them deeply in the resulting accuracy of financial records.

This section of the Act strives to ensure that accurate records are maintained in the years following an audit. One of the most relevant requirements of the Act is that all information related to audit reports must be maintained for a minimum of seven years. The aim of this section is to preserve the details should an audit report's conclusion require verification at a later date.

As an offshoot of this section, there is the implied requirement that CPA firms establish a process and system for the retention and destruction of documents and data. This system must take into account not only the actual financial records, but also documentation of any changes to those records.

Although not specified within the wording of Section 103, it is advisable that the companies themselves also maintain such records. Doing so ensures that there is a reasonable level of security should errors or misrepresentations occur through the accounting firm.

In this way, Section 103, although directed at public accounting firms, is still highly applicable to SOX-compliant companies and their members.

IN THE REAL WORLD

Foreign Public Accounting Firms

The scope of SOX is not limited to U.S.-based companies. Instead, compliance with the Act is mandated for all publicly traded companies on U.S. markets, whether they are U.S. based or foreign.

This requirement has resulted in a strain on the relationship that foreign companies have with the U.S. markets because SOX compliance often competes with their own national regulations and customs.

Further broadening the reach of SOX is the fact that those non-U.S. accounting firms that audit companies required to comply with SOX

IN THE REAL WORLD (CONTINUED)

must also comply. This means that the provisions of Section 103 and all other relevant sections are applicable to those accounting firms.

Additionally, according to SOX Section 106, foreign accounting firms are subject to registrations with the Public Company Accounting Oversight Board (PCAOB). Included are not only those accounting firms that directly audit the publicly traded companies, but also those that submit audit work that the primary auditor relies on.

Section 201: Services Outside the Scope of Practice of Auditors

One of the major contributors to several corporate scandals of the 1990s was a failure on the part of the accounting firms to distance themselves and their auditors sufficiently from those companies that they were hired to audit. By becoming involved in tasks beyond auditing, these firms created conflicts of interest and became entangled in the ensuing scandals.

SOX Section 201 creates limiting criteria on the tasks and services that auditing firms can provide for those companies that they audit. The goal of this clause, and its enforcement, is to prevent accounting firm involvement in fraudulent activities and facilitate their abilities to notice when misrepresentations in financial reporting occur.

Although this section provides a list of services that are considered outside the scope of an auditor's prescribed function, it also maintains the PCAOB's ability to expand the list or create exemptions. Thus, the

PCAOB can adapt this section to new, currently unthought-of activities that may create conflicts of interest.

The list of prohibited services under SOX Section 201 serves to encompass all expert services unrelated to the conduct of the actual audit. These services include:

- Bookkeeping
- Accounting record or financial statement services
- Financial information systems design/implementation
- Appraisal services
- Fairness opinions
- Contribution-in-kind reports
- Actuarial services
- Internal audit outsourcing services
- Management functions or human resources
- Broker, dealer, investment advisor, or investment banking services
- Legal services
- All other expert services unrelated to the audit

One of the most direct impacts of this section is that the external auditor is unable to communicate compliance expectations to the company. Although the auditor may have a clear idea of whether the company will pass or fail the audit, he or she is not able to express concerns; to do so would be tantamount to consulting and therefore be classified as a prohibited activity.

Since the inception of SOX, the companies and firms involved have been able to adapt to the requirements of this section by having some firms consult for some companies and audit others. By dividing the tasks between two separate firms, publicly traded companies are able to retain sufficient autonomy of the auditors, while still receiving the consulting services and advice that they require.

Section 302: Corporate Responsibility for Financial Reports

Amid the scandals of the 1990s, there was a great sense of public frustration with the lack of accountability in corporations. Terms such as "faceless corporation" and "guiltless business" were commonly used to refer to the fact that no one was willing to accept responsibility for the entity's actions. The concept of a business that becomes so large and fragmented that no human is responsible for its actions is a thought that has scared many shareholders as well as the general public.

SOX, in firmly placing responsibility on the shoulders of the chief executive officer (CEO) and chief financial officer (CFO), has worked to abolish this fear. By establishing a clear line of accountability, the Act offers reassurance to the public that corporations do not have a free card for unethical behavior.

In a direct effort to prevent the release of misrepresentative financial information, SOX Section 302 establishes requirements regarding the protection of document integrity. This section explains that internal procedures must be designed and established to ensure that all financial disclosures are complete and accurate.

Such a mandate is prescribed through this section by assigning responsibility for the accuracy and integrity of financial reports to the company's executive officers. In particular, this section requires that both the CEO and the CFO provide a statement that certifies the accuracy of the financial statements and other related disclosures. This statement is to accompany all company audits.

June Proposals

In July 2002, the SEC adopted what has become known as the June Proposals.[1] These proposals have expanded Section 302 by establishing the New Exchange Act Rules 13a-14 and 15d-14. The expansions now require that the CEO and CFO certify the effectiveness of their internal controls not only when submitting a company audit, but also when submitting many SEC reports. This requirement further stipulates that the certification must occur within 90 days before issuing the report.

IN THE REAL WORLD

Impact of New Exchange Act Rules 13a-14 and 15d-14 on Other Companies and Organizations

- *Foreign issuers.* Under other circumstances, Exchange Act Rules are not relevant to foreign issuers. However, because Section 302 applies to foreign issuers, the requirements of these Exchange Act Rules also apply.

In The Real World (continued)

- *Banks and savings associations.* The CEO and CFO of banks and savings associations are required to comply with the requirements of SOX Section 302 if they also file periodic reports under Rules 13a-14 or 15d-14 of the Exchange Act.
- *Small businesses.* Only those small businesses that file Exchange Reports under Rules 13a-14 or 15d-14 are subject to certification requirements.

According to SOX Section 302 and New Exchange Act Rules 13a-14 and 15d-14, the company's CEO and CFO must certify that:

- Controls have been designed, implemented, and tested to ensure the integrity of the financial and related information issued in the quarterly and annual reports. Also, that they are personally certifying that these controls have been effective and that the information is accurate.
- They are responsible for the establishment, maintenance, and evaluation of internal controls. As a direct consequence, the CEO and CFO are culpable should any internal controls be found to have insufficiencies.
- They have presented all information regarding the efficacy of those controls and any significant changes that have been made in their quarterly and annual reports. The requirement that the CEO and CFO verify either that no changes have been made or that they have disclosed the nature of any relevant changes is meant to ensure that investors are provided with only up-to-date information.

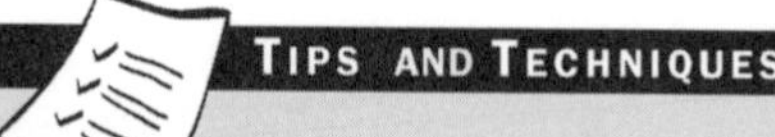

TIPS AND TECHNIQUES

Reports Subject to Certification Requirement

Section 302 of SOX mandates that CEOs and CFOs certify that their company's documents are accurate. This section also requires that they assume responsibility for any discrepancies. Through the June Proposals, the SEC has expanded the scope of SOX Section 302. As a result, statements from the CEO and CFO must accompany several reports submitted through their commission.

Statements certifying that effective controls have been established and tested to ensure the accuracy of the information included in the report must be included with these SEC filings:

- Form 10-K
- Form 10-KSB
- Form 20-F
- Form 40-F
- Form 10-Q
- Form 10-QSB

The expansion of the certification requirement is also applicable to all of the amendments or transition reports that are related to the listed forms.

By creating this requirement, SOX hopes to ensure that there is accountability within publicly traded companies, thereby eliminating the belief that corporations are unable to accept blame for their actions. The goal of expanding Section 302 is to ensure the integrity of all financial reports and provide comprehensive application of accountability.

The SEC did not include Form 6-K and Form 8-K in its requirements, which means that no such certification is required to accompany

Tips and Techniques (continued)

their filing. It is important to note, however, that these forms still carry the requirement that the disclosure controls and procedures have been designed, maintained, and evaluated. The only difference is that CEO/CFO certification of their responsibility for those procedures is not required.

Public Dissent

One of the greatest concerns of SOX in general is that cost of compliance outweighs the benefits. Although the price tag associated with the endeavor does appear to lessen in later years, several companies are still disgruntled by the costs incurred during the early years.

The costs associated with SOX Section 302 compliance are matched by those of Section 404 compliance. This fact has caused a great many disgruntled conversations among those who believe that SOX compliance is too expensive.

Further difficulty with Section 302 stems from the fact that it requires CEOs and CFOs to certify and take responsibility for processes and controls they did not design. It is rare that a corporate executive will have enough background or education in information technology (IT) to be able to design such controls personally, yet they are held personally responsible.

The solution that many have employed has come to be known as subcertification whereby process specialist designs the controls and certifies their effectiveness, before the CEO and CFO. Although this does provide some reassurance for the corporate executives, it is not meant to diminish their responsibility nor pass on their culpability.

Outside of the corporate world, there has been some public dissent against the fact that this section carries a penalty only if the violation can be proven to have been knowingly and intentionally committed. This is unlike other SOX sections, which carry lesser penalties for unwilling violations.

Section 404: Management Assessment of Internal Controls

Section 404 of SOX can be credited with creating most of the Act's controversy. As the Act's most widely termed and broadly spread section, Section 404 tends to consume the majority of first-year compliance efforts and resources.

After implementation and throughout SOX's first year, many corporations found themselves pressed to meet the requirements of Section 404 because they initially underestimated the breadth of its scope. Upon discovering the nature of the efforts that would be required to comply with this section, several corporations found that doing so required a significant increase in both their budgets and personnel resources.

In general, this section requires that all annual financial reports include an Internal Control Report to certify and explain those efforts that have been made to ensure the integrity and accuracy of the financial information.

Requirements of Section 404 Internal Control Report

In compliance with SOX Section 404, each annual report must include a statement by executive officers to the effect that they are responsible for the establishment and maintenance of the internal control structure and other procedures for financial reporting. In addition, the Internal Control Report must also include an assessment of all internal controls related to the financial information that has been released. This assessment is required to inform investors not only about the structure of the controls, but also about their efficacy.

Requirements of the Executive Officers

In complying with SOX Section 404, the executive officers (CEO and CFO) must certify a document that contains these statements and information:

- *Statement of responsibility for establishing and maintaining internal financial reporting controls.* This statement is similar to that which is required by SOX Section 302 and certifies that the CEO/CFO assumes responsibility and culpability should the internal financial reporting controls not meet standards.

  By placing the responsibility for the establishment of such controls at the top of the company's hierarchy, SOX is working to ensure that those with the most power also have the greatest responsibility.
- *An explanation of the framework used to evaluate the efficacy of internal financial reporting controls.* This document serves to educate investors and all other applicable parties about those controls that have been implemented within the company. This information must itself be up-to-date, complete, and accurate.

  For some investors, certification itself will not be enough to offer assurance that the financial records are accurate. There needs to be a paper trail that establishes evidence of this fact. By reporting on the framework used to test the controls, companies create a transparent system that fosters investor confidence.

- *Report on assessment results of internal financial reporting controls for the most recent fiscal year.* In addition to explaining the nature of the internal controls, this document must attest to the fact that these controls have been tested recently and must provide the results of the assessment. This requirement further ensures that the company has taken every measure to ensure the accuracy of the report's information.

  It is not enough that controls are established; they must be checked and tested routinely to ensure their ongoing efficacy. As the company changes and evolves, these routine tests become even more vital.

- *Report disclosing significant deficiencies that could result in misstatement.* Finally, the document must release any gaps within the control framework that could result in a misstatement of the financial information. It is understood that no system can ever offer perfect protection, but when significant risks are present, they must be reported.

  By mandating such a practice, SOX ensures that investors have a complete picture of the company's control system and its efficacy. Depending on their severity, these deficiencies could nullify the CEO/CFO's certification that the internal controls are effective and that the reported information is accurate.

In addition to the executive officers' certification that their controls are effective, the auditor must provide a statement to the same effect. By requiring the auditor to second the executive officers' certification, SOX provides multiple levels of checks and balances.

Steps toward Section 404 Compliance

Although compliance with Section 404 must be integrated into an entire SOX compliance plan, certain strategies are geared specifically to this section.

Companies generally proceed with SOX compliance by adopting an internal control framework. Key aspects of this process that are directly related to Section 404 include:

- *Assessment and improvement of internal controls.* The first step of any action must always be the development of a plan. By taking inventory of current internal controls, the company is able to identify deficiencies and isolate any areas that create threats to the accuracy of its documents. Included in this step is the development and implementation of plans to either improve or redo the faulty components (see Exhibit 3.1).

EXHIBIT 3.1

Companies Must Take Many Steps to Achieve Compliance with Section 404 of SOX.

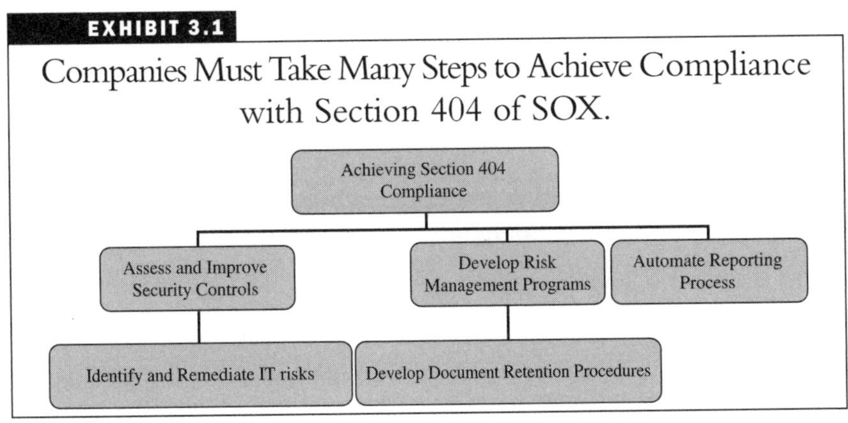

- *Development of risk management programs.* Ensuring the integrity of financial reports requires the identification of all potential opportunities for misrepresentation and error. A risk management program seeks to offer preventions and solutions to help minimize the possibility that such errors or frauds could occur. The primary component of any risk management program is the establishment of internal controls that protect the integrity of company data and documents.
- *Automation of reporting processes.* Essentially, automation of reporting processes is a safeguard to protect the final stages of report creation. By automating reporting processes, companies are able to limit the danger of human error and improve efficiency. They also limit the opportunities for purposeful human manipulation of the data.
- *Identification and remediation of IT risks.* IT is integral to the activities of any organization. The problem is that IT systems found within companies are large, complicated, and often disorganized. This fact provides several exploitable weaknesses that could adversely affect the accuracy of financial reports. For this reason, a large portion of risk identification must be focused specifically on the company's IT systems.
- *Development of document retention procedures.* Documentation is an integral part of SOX compliance. Not only does Section 404 mandate that financial records be maintained and secured, it also requires that control procedure design and testing documents be maintained. By establishing a clear paper trail, companies are able to follow up on control

inefficiencies and identify the weak points for quicker remediation.

Exemption from Section 404

In light of separate industry-specific regulation that applies to them, under SOX Section 405, all registered investment companies are exempt from the provisions of Sections 401, 402, and 404. In addition, these companies are also exempt from the implications of any amendments to these sections or the rules of the SEC under these sections.

TIPS AND TECHNIQUES

Pitfalls to Avoid in Achieving Section 404 Compliance

The lessons of SOX's first year have taught the corporate world that it is possible to meet compliance requirements without undermining alternate company goals. By avoiding these pitfalls, a company can make a concerted effort to ensure that their business interests are not put on the back burner while they comply with SOX:

- *Do not defer system implementations.* It can be tempting to defer system implementations to avoid either the cost or having to report on the changes made. It is not advisable to do so, however, because that would be putting compliance first and potentially compromising the business's efficiency and existence.
- *Do not compromise efficiency by relying on manual controls rather than application controls.* It is clear that automated controls

Tips and Techniques (continued)

are preferable wherever they can be applied. Not only do automated controls facilitate a business's efficiency, they also aid in SOX compliance by limiting human error.

- *Do not fail to evaluate control designs prior to developing compliancy tests.* Before developing a test to ensure that controls are working effectively, a company should evaluate the control designs. This can help catch deficiencies early, before the costly tests.

Section 406: Code of Ethics for Senior Financial Officers

Section 406 of SOX puts forth the requirement that all senior financial officers be bound by a company-specific code of ethics. The purpose of this section is to ensure that all senior officials understand, from the start, the expectations that they are required to meet.

A code of ethics also serves as a vehicle for educating members about the compliance efforts that the company is making by including relevant clauses such as "Conflicts of Interest," "Honesty and Fairness," and "Reporting Unethical Behavior."

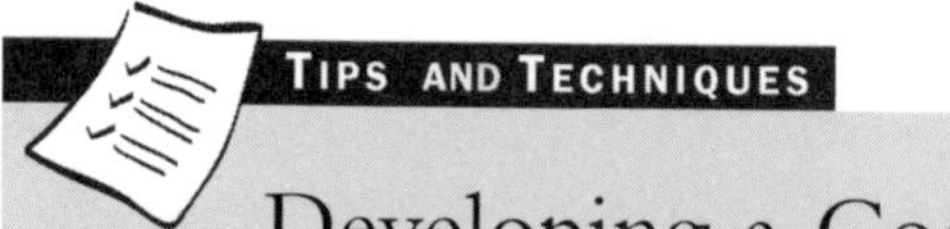

Developing a Code of Ethics

The code of ethics that a company designs will be unique to the specific nature of that company. There are several standard components, however, that most codes will include.

Tips and Techniques (continued)

Although SOX requires only the creation of a code of ethics for executive members, it may be advisable to create an alternate code for other company members and employees. Ensuring a culture of ethical behavior is an important step toward SOX compliance.

Some components of an effective code of ethics for executive officers include (see Exhibit 3.2):

EXHIBIT 3.2

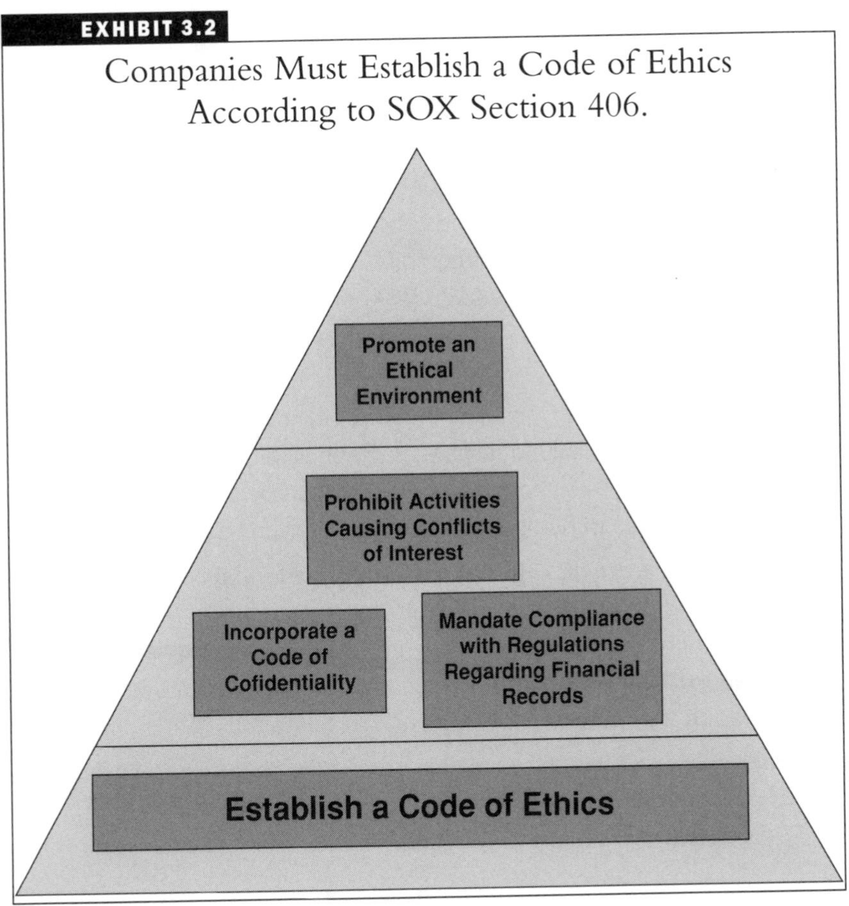

Tips and Techniques (continued)

- *Cover page with statement of values.* The cover page should serve to identify that this is an official code of ethics. It should also express the general values held up by the company. The values that should be included are integrity and accountability, safety, respect, fairness, honesty, and innovation.
- *Introduction.* The introduction will include a call for all employees to adhere to an ethical standard that includes loyalty to the company, compliance with all relevant laws, and observance of general moral standards. The introduction should also explain why the code is important. Finally, there should be a statement to the effect that the code of ethics is not exhaustive and company members should use well-guided judgment to make decisions or seek guidance.
- *Financial records.* This section concerns the maintenance and integrity of accounting records and financial reports. It clarifies that the company expects compliance with generally accepted accounting principles (GAAP), SOX, and other regulations.
- *Conflict of interest.* A code of ethics should include the prohibition of all activities or circumstances that result in a conflict of interest including improper conduct, noncompany compensation, influential gifts, and financial interests in other businesses. This section should also include prohibition of personal use of company assets or opportunities.
- *Code of confidentiality.* The code of confidentiality should reflect the confidentiality requirements unique to the company and the industry in which it functions. This section can reference relevant laws and regulations, such as the Health Insurance Portability and Accountability Act HIPAA.
- *Promotion of an ethical environment.* This important section concerns the promotion of ethical compliance within the company and among employees. The section includes

Tips and Techniques (continued)

guidance on the reporting of violations, both for the person reporting and the one receiving the report.

In terms of format, a code of ethics should be written in a positive tone. It should be as concise and brief as possible, providing for quick referencing. Finally, the code should make reference to other polices and documents that are relevant, providing alternate resources in times of uncertainty.

Section 409: Real Time Issuer Disclosures

This section provides direction to issuers to disclose relevant financial information on a rapid and current basis. Although the requirements were in place pre-SOX, Section 409 expands on the circumstances in which they are required.

The purpose of this disclosure is to ensure that if a major event occurs between the issuance of quarterly reports, investors will have the information in enough time to make sound decisions. Without it, investors would be forced to rely on quarterly reports that could be inaccurate and out of date.

At the start of the compliance effort, this section was referred to as the Y2K equivalent because the clause appeared to require significant technological advancements and implications, much like preparing for Y2K did. Although the section initially created a great deal of panic among companies worried about the requirements and related costs, these fears have been greatly unfounded. Compliance with the SEC Section 409 Guidelines has not required drastic and costly IT changes.

In order to meet the demands of Section 409, a company must file Form 8-K whenever a major disruption occurs that could create a material impact on the company's financial situation. Although there are several situations in which the filing of this form are required, they are all major and the requirement of their disclosure should not come as a surprise. The requirement that companies file a Form 8-K existed well before the inception of SOX. The pre-SOX requirements that mandated such a filing included:

- Changes in company control
- Acquisition or disposition of significant assets
- Bankruptcy or receivership
- Certifying accountant changes
- Director resignation
- Code of ethics modifications

Through Section 409, SOX has served to expand on these requirements to further protect the interests of investors and ensure that they receive only up-to-date information. Post-SOX additions include:

- Entry into a material agreement that is not in the ordinary course of business
- Termination of a material course agreement that is not ordinary
- Creation of a material obligation under an off–balance sheet arrangement
- Triggering events that accelerate or decrease a direct financial obligation or off–balance sheet arrangement
- Costs associated with exit or disposal activities

- Material impairments
- Failure to satisfy a continued listing rule or standard
- Changes or restatements of previously issued financial statements, related audit reports, or completed interim reviews

In addition to these circumstances, others were included in original drafts but not on the final list. These events do not require the filing of Form 8-K:

- Changes to employee benefit and stock ownership plans
- Loss of a major customer

IN THE REAL WORLD

Maneuverability in Section 409

SOX Section 409 has created additional circumstances in which companies must submit SEC Form 8-Ks. The purpose of these forms is to provide timely information to investors when events occur that could create significant impacts on the company's financial figures.

One circumstance that requires the submission of Form 8-K is the situation in which an issuer breaks an agreement that creates an increase in the company's financial obligations. This circumstance was included on the SEC Guideline list because such a situation could reasonably create a significant impact on the company's financial state.

It is important to note, however, that this requirement stipulates that disclosure needs to occur only once the agreement is broken. This means that even if the company has a clear indication that the situation will occur, it is not required to disclose that suspicion.

In The Real World (continued)

There is also a great deal of ambiguity regarding the circumstances that mandate a Form 8-K submission. The use of the term ''material'' in many of the descriptions has led to the belief that this section will pose implementation difficulties.

Section 806: Protection for Employees of Publicly Traded Companies Who Provide Evidence of Fraud

This section of the SOX seeks to offer protection for whistle-blowers, thereby facilitating the disclosure of illegal or unethical activities. Essentially this section recognizes that the PCAOB and SEC cannot effectively identify all transgressions without the assistance of those within the company or accounting firms.

In the Real World

Enron's Whistle-Blower, Sherron Watkins

Sherron Watkins, a former vice president of Enron Corporation, is the much-contested whistle-blower in the 2001 Enron scandal.

In August 2001, she sent an electronic message to Enron chairman Kenneth Lay warning him of potential dissentions within the company. Although this email was the ultimate key that led to the uncovering of the Enron scandal, it did not do so for more than five months.

There are two camps regarding Watkins and whether she deserves the distinction of ''whistle-blower.'' On one hand, *Time* magazine

IN THE REAL WORLD (CONTINUED)

has hailed her as one of the "People of 2002"; [2] on the other, *Forbes* magazine has claimed that although she had the whistle, she "blew it."

Those who support Watkins argue that she went through the appropriate in-house channels after suspecting accounting irregularities. Those who disagree argue that Watkins's email simply attempted to warn those responsible for the fraud that they were in danger of being caught. They assert that had she actually sought to function as a whistle-blower, she would have alerted the public.

Essentially, the truth hinges on Watkins's state of mind and understanding of Lay's involvement at the time that she wrote the email. Watkins has stated that her objective was to save Enron before it was too late.

Irrespective of her motivation or objectives, Watkins's email directly contributed to the ultimate creation of SOX. Now many are wondering whether that same act, particularly Section 806, would have changed the outcome of the Enron scandal had it existed earlier.

This section serves to encourage those with knowledge of illegal or unethical behaviors to come forward by prohibiting any actions that could be taken against them by their company or other organizations.

Activities Prohibited by Section 806

SOX Section 806 speaks to company members who would try to dissuade or punish a whistle-blower in order to prevent the person from coming forward. The section formally prohibits the discharge, demotion, suspension, threatening, harassing, or otherwise discriminating against any and all company employees who provide assistance to investigations related to shareholder fraud.

The goal of this section is to protect whistle-blowers and lessen the consequences that many face in opting to go public with information of unethical or illegal activities. In doing so, this section hopes to facilitate whistle-blower actions with the understanding that those within a company often have greater insights into a company's actions.

Violation Penalties

This section also provides express directions regarding how to handle someone who violates the penalty and how the whistle-blowing employee should be compensated. It is important to know that should employees or former employees seek to allege violation of Section 806, they must do so within 90 days of the violation.

If an employee suffers under any of those actions prohibited by this section, the offended employee may seek and be awarded restitutions including:

- Reinstatement of employment to level that would have been achieved if not for the discrimination
- Back pay with interest
- Special damages compensation, including litigation costs, expert witness fees, and reasonable attorney fees

WorldCom's Whistle-Blower, Cynthia Cooper

Whistle-blowers tend to hold a precarious position in the public eye. They are often touted as do-gooders who bravely put their careers on the line for the betterment of the public good. Yet they are also held to a higher standard than most, and the public can be quick to withdraw their support.

As the vice president of Internal Audit at WorldCom, Cynthia Cooper conducted a secret investigation based on her suspicion of accounting irregularities. She reported the results of her investigations, which uncovered $3.9 billion in inflated profits, to WorldCom's board of directors.

Although some have commended her actions and called her a brave whistle-blower, others argue that she worked only based on self-interest. Those who do not agree that Cynthia Cooper is a true whistle-blower claim that while she uncovered the scandal, she did not expose it to the public, but rather kept the information within the company for several months.

Conclusion

This chapter has discussed some of the biggest issues that arise from SOX by examining key sections of the legislation. It is worth repeating that although these sections can be examined individually to provide an overview of the Act, all sections are relevant and must be complied with in order achieve full SOX compliance.

The goal of this chapter was to provide not only just an overview, but also a clear indication of the consequences created by each section and the specific requirements that will lead to successful compliance.

Some of the important concepts that were explained in this section include:

- SOX is applicable not only to publicly traded companies, but also those professionals who audit them. In order to maintain the integrity of external audits and prevent any conflicts of interest, Section 201 mandates that auditors refrain from providing any services external to their role in the audits.
- One of the largest goals of SOX was to provide the public and the legal community with a "blamable" entity, should some aspect of a company's financial reporting system go awry. Section 302 serves to fulfill this goal by firmly placing the responsibility for the protection of financial documents and their accuracy with the CEO and CFO of the publicly traded company.
- Similar to the requirements of Section 302, Section 404 also demands that the company CEO/CFO affirm their responsibilities within the company. This section requires that management certify the efficacy of internal controls and include such certification within their annual report.
- When it comes to compliance, the tone from the top is one of the strongest motivators for success. When company executives are held to a high ethical standard, the rest of the company is more likely to follow suit. SOX Section 406 requires that companies

establish a clear code of ethics for executive officers to ensure that they understand the expectations that they must meet.

- In keeping with the SOX goal of providing shareholders with complete and accurate information, Section 409 expands the list of circumstances under which SEC Form 8-Ks must be submitted. These forms serve to update shareholders of any significant events that could influence financial figures during the time between quarterly reports.
- Section 806 offers protection to whistle-blowers and seeks to promote the reporting of unethical or illegal activities from within the company. This section clearly indicates those actions that cannot be taken to dissuade whistle-blowing and lays out the penalties that companies could face if they are in violation.

For more information on other sections of the Sarbanes-Oxley Act, refer to the Appendix in this book.

Summary

- Section 103 requires that public accounting firms maintain accurate records on the companies they serve for a minimum of seven years.
- Section 201 mandates that auditors limit the scope of their contact with those companies they audit.
- Section 302 requires that internal controls be established to protect document integrity and that the company CEO/CFO assume responsibility for such actions.

- Section 404 mandates that the CEO/CFO certify the establishment and efficacy of internal controls related to their financial reports.
- Section 409 requires that the company establish a code of ethics to guide senior financial officers.
- Section 806 offers protection to whistle-blowers by clearly indicating that such actions cannot be retaliated against and that companies that dissuade whistle-blowing activities will face consequences.

Notes

1. More information regarding the June Proposals and other SEC information can be found at www.sec.gov.
2. *Time,* December 22, 2002.

CHAPTER 4

Implementing a Strategy

After reading this chapter, you will be able to:

- Understand some of the challenges that companies face in achieving compliance.
- Understand the steps in designing and implementing a Sarbanes-Oxley Act (SOX) compliance plan.
- Understand the impact that Public Company Accounting Oversight Board (PCAOB) Audit Standard No. 2 has on publicly traded companies and those firms that audit them.

Introduction

Outside of the theoretical and philosophical implications that the Sarbanes-Oxley Act (SOX) has for companies, the U.S. economy, and the global market, there are practical considerations to compliance. Designing and implementing a strategy for SOX compliance is an exercise in problem solving and balancing resources for many companies. By starting early, newly listed companies can provide themselves with ample time to establish their plan and revise it if necessary.

TIPS AND TECHNIQUES

Creating the Right Mentality

Part of establishing a culture of compliance in a company involves creating the right mentality among company members (see Exhibit 4.1). This applies to everyone, executives as well as nonexecutives.

- *Management must take personal ownership of the compliance effort.* In order to ensure that compliance efforts are taken seriously by all company members, the message from the top must be unwavering in every action.
- *The company cannot treat compliance as a one-time event.* If compliance is treated as a one-time event, companies will establish short-term solutions without considering long-term compliance efforts that could save money and resources.
- *All company members need to understand the compliance efforts.* Instead of simply establishing and implementing controls, management should make a concerted effort to educate company members about the importance of compliance and the efforts being made to ensure compliance.
- *Ethics training should be included in both initial employee training and annually.* Although SOX compliance requires a code of ethics only for executives, creating such a code for all members of the company will help establish clear guidelines and enforce the culture of compliance.

EXHIBIT 4.1

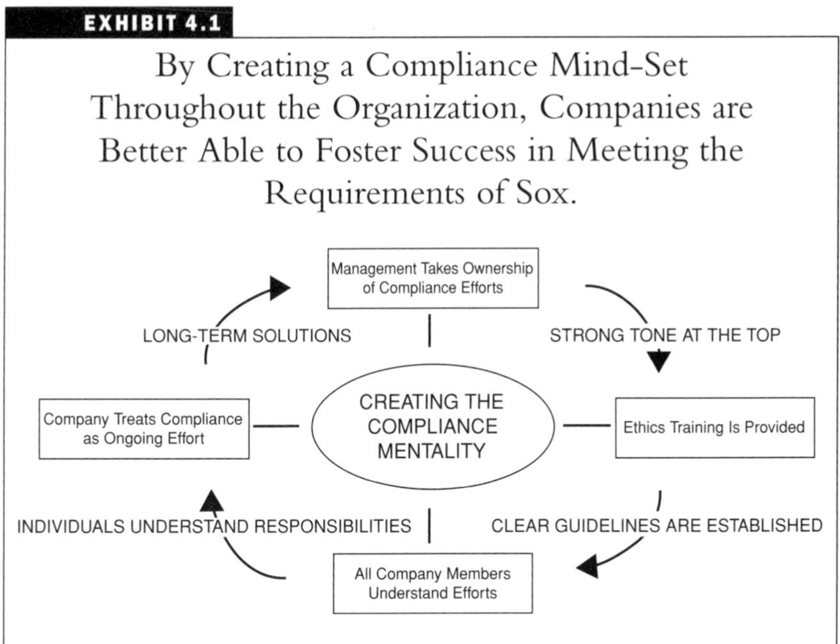

Challenges of Compliance

Most companies that have implemented the mandates of SOX have found that a large part of compliance is problem solving. One of the greatest challenges associated with SOX is not understanding what the compliance itself entails.

Unfortunately, SOX itself does not provide detailed guidelines for how to comply. Although very clear on the expectations of what the end result must be, SOX does not elucidate the steps toward compliance or even the specific criteria that must be met.

Taking it one step further, SOX also prohibits auditors from providing hands-on assistance to companies in their compliance efforts. This stipulation is a part of the Act's objective to limit the internal roles that auditors take on within the companies.

Additionally, yet another compliance challenge that some companies are having difficulties with is distinguishing what constitutes a "material" or "significant" issue. Neither SOX nor additional SEC regulations offer much guidance in directing companies and their executives to interpret these ambiguous terms.

The problem arises when companies must identify which processes pose material threats to the integrity of their financial reports. Without clear definitions, the companies are left guessing, and many have found that they are either over or under complying.

One solution to this challenge is for companies to look to outside regulations, requirements, and guidelines for direction. For example, financial records that do not comply with generally accepted accounting principles (GAAP) can be considered significant and serve as a warning flag that this is an area requiring further attention.

A lot of confusion has also been generated over what the difference is between internal controls of Sections 302 and 404. Some companies have found it difficult to distinguish between them, and this has led to inefficiencies in their compliance efforts.

The Securities and Exchange Commission (SEC) has made an effort to clarify this ambiguity. In Section 302, the internal controls are meant to describe the procedures that have been put in place to ensure that the chief executive officer (CEO) and chief financial officer (CFO) understand and are able to monitor their company's information. These controls are relevant to the accuracy of such SEC reports as Forms 10-K and 10-Q. However, the use of the term "internal controls" in Section 404 refers to control over the company's financial information and its accuracy. Essentially, these controls are meant to ensure that the company remains compliant with GAAP.

Finally, companies have found the cost of compliance a significant challenge in their SOX efforts. Between hiring consultants, purchasing new software and technology, reorganizing systems, and establishing an internal audit committee, most companies have felt the financial pinch.

Of course, these costs were significantly greater in the first year than in subsequent ones for those companies that established long-term goals compliance plans. One-time costs, such as software purchases and system reorganization, do not recur in later years, and companies have also been able to decrease the price tag of compliance as their systems and efforts have become more efficient.

IN THE REAL WORLD

Generally Accepted Accounting Principles

GAAP provides procedures and standards to guide companies as they assemble their financial statements. These regulations encompass the collective policies of several organizations including the:

- American Accounting Association
- American Institute of Certified Public Accountants
- Financial Accounting Standards Board
- Institute of Management Accountants
- Securities and Exchange Commission

The prime objective of these standards is to provide a common reporting system so that investors have a platform for company comparison.

IN THE REAL WORLD (CONTINUED)

GAAP is frequently referred to in regard to compliance with SEC regulations and SOX. Without incorporating GAAP, a company cannot hope to comply with any regulations requiring accuracy in its financial records.

Strategy Outline

Efforts toward compliance with the regulations of SOX can be placed into a general outline, such as the one found in this section. However, the unique process for each company will be dictated by its specific circumstances, and no two strategies will be identical.

IN THE REAL WORLD

PepsiCo Evaluates Its Culture of Compliance

As is recommended for sustainable compliance, PepsiCo has made a concerted effort to instill an overall culture of compliance among all divisions and members of the company.[a]

In order to continually adapt and evaluate its efforts, PepsiCo enlists its internal auditors to conduct surveys and gather information regarding compliance in activities such as:

- Hiring practices
- Employee evaluation
- Contract solicitation

In The Real World (continued)

- Incident reporting
- Objective setting

These surveys can then be used to evaluate and adapt efforts at establishing effective measures to control the tone from the top.

[a] Stephen Wagner and Lee Dittmar, "The Unexpected Benefits of Sarbanes-Oxley," *Harvard Business Review* (April 2006).

Step 1: Plan

After collecting requirements from the auditor, a preliminary plan can be developed that includes risk identification and assessment. To achieve this, companies will identify those processes and activities that offer exploitable vulnerabilities with the potential to affect financial statements.

The identification of risks should be done first at the entity level and be broken up either by division or location. This identification includes an in-depth consideration of entity-level controls including:

- *Organizational complexity.* The organization of the company and the hierarchy of company members will affect both the establishment of controls and the identification of risks. As a result, the overall layout and complexity of the company and its systems needs to be considered. Any anomalies that could present difficulties for plan implementation, such as missing management or foreign subsidiaries, also need to be considered and accounted for.
- *Policies and procedures.* In order to clearly identify risk areas, the company must first clearly identify all policies and procedures that can have a direct impact on the accuracy of financial reports.

By identifying and cataloging these policies and procedures, the company will be in a better position to understand where its control creation efforts must be focused. This stage of the planning creates an opportunity to limit control development, thereby establishing greater efficiency and better cost management.

- *Segregation of duties.* A major component of the establishment of controls is that each activity that can affect financial records be protected by a system of checks and balances. It is vital to the integrity of financial information that there are no dead ends in the chain of control.

  This means ensuring that no one individual has unreasonable powers and authorities within the company. Some form of watchdog must be established in every situation to protect against errors or misrepresentations.

  By evaluating the current state of the segregation of duties, the company can better assess the requirements that it will need to ensure that a system of checks and balances exists.
- *Fraud prevention.* Although it would be nice to think that all financial misrepresentations are the result of preventable error, it is important that companies not ignore the fact that fraud happens. In order to secure the integrity of financial information adequately, a company must identify all processes that pose potential opportunities for fraudulent manipulation.
- *IT environment.* The information technology (IT) division of a company plays an integral role in the establishment of security measures to protect the accuracy of financial documents. The goal of evaluating the company's IT environment is to identify

which entities or processes contain controls that will need to be documented and tested.

This evaluation also provides companies with the ability to identify opportunities to improve their IT technology and software in order to better facilitate efficient processes.

- *High-level financial statement review processes.* The last checkpoint for financial information must be the most secure from manipulation because there will be no further checks to verify its accuracy and catch misrepresentations. As a result, the high-level financial statement review process needs to be evaluated meticulously.
- *Tone at the top.* It is recognized that if management and executives do not buy in to the compliance efforts, then the company will find little success in their implementation. Right from the planning stage, the company should monitor the "tone at the top" and implement any changes required to improve it.

Tips and Techniques

Demonstrating the Tone at the Top

As part of SOX compliance, companies are required to document internal controls that have been established. Documenting those controls that govern the attitudes and behaviors of management and other high-level employees can be achieved through:

- *Meeting minutes for strategic meetings, board meetings, committee meetings, and so forth.* These documents will demonstrate that compliance is on the agenda and is being

Tips and Techniques (continued)

considered with every relevant discussion and decision that is made.

- *Internal audit memos to the audit committee.* Memos that reflect conscious efforts to facilitate compliance efforts are a clear indication that executives have signed on to the compliance effort.
- *Formal executive and company communications with employees.* When executives are working on SOX compliance, they need to actively create a culture of compliance within every area of the company. Handbooks, newsletters, bulletins, and other formal company communications should reflect this objective.
- *Salary, promotion, and compensation history of high-level employees.* A company that values compliance will value those employees who embody those efforts. As such, salary, promotion, and compensation history will demonstrate the type of people and behaviors that the company rewards.
- *Ethics codes and their implementation.* SOX mandates that an executive code of ethics be established, but many companies will go further and establish similar codes for all company members.
- *Employee hiring processes and evaluations.* Compliance success is directly related to those people involved. Hiring practices created to consider skills, abilities, and experiences relevant to SOX demonstrate that the company is committed to compliance efforts.

The efforts and attitudes of management, executives, and board members create a running effect throughout the company and throughout the company's compliance effort.

By establishing a culture of compliance, the company will further its chances of SOX success and ensure that all company members are involved in the effort.

Step 2: Establish a Control Framework

The second stage of SOX compliance is the establishment of a control framework. This is the developmental stage in which solutions are identified for each of the key risk areas that were identified in the planning stage. It is common at this point for a company to enlist the assistance of outsourced experts such as certified public accountants (CPAs).

To develop an effective framework, the company must go through each risk area and identify its function, its key process, and the control objective that will eliminate or minimize the risk.

Step 3: Design Specific Controls

For each control objective that was identified in the previous step, a control must now be designed. Essentially, controls can be manual or automated, and can be preventive or detective. In order to meet the risk requirements of each targeted process effectively, the action steps for every control need to be documented effectively.

TIPS AND TECHNIQUES

Common Controls

One of the major steps in any SOX compliance strategy is the establishment of controls to safeguard those processes that have been identified as posing significant risk. Although the identifiable areas of risk are unique for each company, every company will have to address some common control themes in order to achieve compliance. These controls include:

- External security controls
- External security change management controls

Tips and Techniques (continued)

- File security
- Control of sensitive financial data
- Testing of backup and restore processes
- Physical access controls
- Data retention policy
- Strategies for investigating and resolving security problems

By focusing their efforts on establishing controls for only those processes that provide material risk to the accuracy of their financial documents, companies will be better able comply with SOX in an efficient and cost-effective manner.

This clear documentation also serves to help identify the steps at which the control should be tested in order to verify its effectiveness. This serves to establish the parameters required to document and test each internal control. These parameters should include not only the test design, but also the frequency at which the test should occur and any potential deficiencies that it may have.

In the Real World

Benefits of Automated Controls

Compliance with SOX requires that companies identify areas of their operations that pose material risks to the accuracy of their financial documents. After doing so, the companies will establish controls to safeguard against such risks and to protect the integrity of their documents against fraud and error.

In The Real World (continued)

Manual processes can be a significant weakness of internal controls because they are prone to mistakes based on human error. Thus, it is recommended that companies establish systems of automated controls. Such systems reduce the involvement of manual processes and thereby limit the likelihood of error. These systems also limit the risk of fraud by eliminating opportunities for human interaction with the data and documentation.

An additional benefit of automated controls is that they provide cost-efficient testing. Since automated controls are consistent, one test is often enough to adequately determine if they are functioning or not. However, the testing of manual controls requires that several tests be conducted to determine the significance of human error.

It is also possible that automated controls will require less frequent testing because SOX compliance can be achieved through the rationalization that no significant changes have occurred that would alter test results. For example, proof that security measures have been established to eliminate unauthorized software modifications would aid in the reasoning that previous tests are still applicable.

Step 4: Document Control Activity

After identifying and implementing the controls, SOX compliance requires that the company document those activities and processes that are performed to ensure that the control objectives are met. The process by which this is done should have been developed during Step 3.

By documenting the control activities, the company is establishing its record that will help in compliance with Section 404 of the Act.

This section requires that control establishment, monitoring, and testing be properly documented and reported. The section also mandates that the CEO/CFO certify the efficacy of the controls, a task that is further supported by this stage.

Step 5: Evaluate Control Design

As an intermediate step before testing the control's effectiveness, the company should evaluate the control design to ensure that it meets the risk prevention objectives laid out in Step 2.

By completing an evaluation of the control design before conducting tests for compliance, the company will be able to identify and remedy problems. This is more efficient and cost effective because it prevents the occurrence of unnecessary control tests.

To evaluate the control design, the company must consider:

- *What the specific control is.* This identifies the risk that is being safeguarded as well as the control that has been designed to protect the integrity and accuracy of the document.
- *Who performs the control activity.* It is important to note which company member performs the control activity and which additional members have access to relevant information. This is important so that when discrepancies occur, there is a record of the control, the related activities, and the company members who are responsible.
- *How the control is performed.* Clearly documenting how the control is performed serves several purposes. First, this goes toward Section 404 compliance that requires that controls be disclosed and certified by the CEO/CFO.

Second, it also helps ensure that the company maintains a clear record of the process and steps. This record will be valuable in situations were the control needs to be reevaluated, changes need to be made, or new company members need to be trained.

- *What reports or other information are used to perform the control.* SOX is very clear in requiring that risk management and control establishment be properly documented. All relevant data and documentation need to be identified and a system for its storage and destruction needs to be established.
- *How frequently the control operates.* Knowing how often the control operates will help in determining not only ability to mitigate risk, but also how best to test the control. Establishing a schedule of testing well in advance is important, especially with those controls that occur infrequently and require large sample sizes for accurate results.
- *Whether the documented control activity meets all of the control objective assertions.* It is imperative that the designed control serves its ascribed function. If it is discovered that this is not the case, then the company is required to retrace its steps and alter the control to ensure that its activity fulfills its objectives.

Step 6: Test Control Effectiveness

This step ensures that each control is operating as designed and as intended by the company. In order for the test to be effective, unbiased testing that is representative of the total population is required. To ensure this, statistical sampling techniques should be used and samples should be randomly selected.

If no exceptions to the control objectives are found, then the control is operating effectively. However, exceptions that are found should be recorded in a remediation log, and the process will start again until the risk process is matched with an effective control.

TIPS AND TECHNIQUES

Strategies to Maximize Control Effectiveness

Every step of SOX compliance offers opportunities to improve efficiency and effectiveness. Some strategies that companies can employ to ensure that their controls are functioning at the top of their capabilities follow.

- *Ensure that all company employees understand their responsibilities related to control activities.* When it comes to SOX, people are the X factor. Well-trained and educated company members can create an environment in which compliance is efficient and highly effective. However, when company members do not understand their role or fail to meet their requirements, the efficacy of the control will crumble. This is why training is imperative to SOX success.
- *Maintain a regular control testing schedule.* Establishing a control testing schedule that reflects the nature of the control, the frequency at which it runs, and its relative risk level can help ensure that problems are identified in a timely manner. By not waiting until the audit deadline to test controls, a company can ensure that it has ample time to make any necessary changes and adaptations to those controls that function in an insufficient capacity.
- *Establish an effective and organized method for control test documentation.* Releasing reports regarding the results of controls tests is a mandatory part of SOX compliance. For this

Tips and Techniques (continued)

reason, it is vital that control test documentation is captured and stored in a strategic manner. A system must also be established so that control test documentation is delivered to relevant parties in a timely fashion. The CEO/CFO who is required to certify these controls must know of the results, but so must those company members who are responsible for designing and implementing changes when the controls fail.

Original PCAOB Audit Standard No. 2

Public Company Accounting Oversight Board (PCAOB) Audit Standard No. 2 (AS No. 2) is the standard for control testing that was approved on June 17, 2004, by the SEC.[1] It requires that auditors release an opinion regarding the internal control effectiveness of all public company clients and also establishes a clear distinction between the roles of company executives and the auditor. By mandating that auditors evaluate internal control effectiveness, this standard provides an extra layer of confidence so that investors can trust the information being presented to them.

The task distinctions that are made by AS No. 2 are not as much extensions of SOX Section 201, but rather a clarification that the auditor's opinion of the internal controls is not the same as the executive's certification of their efficacy.

AS No. 2 stipulates that executives must:

- Maintain responsibility for the internal control system's efficacy.
- Take appropriate steps to evaluate the effectiveness of internal controls by implementing a recognized control criteria framework.

- Support their evaluation with all necessary documentation.
- Create a written assessment regarding the efficacy findings at the end of each fiscal year.

It mandates that auditors must:

- Discover and assess the executive's evaluation process.
- Plan and conduct an internal control audit.
- Create an opinion on the management's written assessment

AS No. 2 further stipulates that executives must *not*:

- Involve auditor testing in their assessment of the efficiency of internal controls.
- Fail to fulfill any part of their responsibilities. To do so would require the auditor to reject the assessment.

Updated PCAOB Audit Standard No. 2

The PCAOB has updated AS No. 2 to make the standard more applicable, easier to comply with, and less of a financial burden. Changes to AS No. 2 were the result of two realizations by the PCAOB:

1. *Auditing internal controls over financial reporting has been a beneficial action.* It has created a culture of corporate governance and has vastly improved the quality and efficiency of company's processes and controls. Furthermore, it has had a positive result on the accuracy of financial reports and has impressed investors with the increased transparency of public companies.
2. *Auditing internal controls over financial reporting has been a costly action.* Companies, already facing the large cost of SOX

compliance, are concerned by the cost of the audits. Many believe that the standard was not written with enough consideration for an efficient and cost-effective audit process.

IN THE REAL WORLD

Case Study: Bandag Tire Co.

Bandag is a manufacturer supplying materials for tire retreading, including tread rubber and other equipment. This company has over 1,000 customers in 100 countries.[a]

Initially, Bandag used Excel spreadsheets for control documentation. After discovering the strategy's deficiencies, Bandag's internal control project manager, Mark Johnson, chose to implement Paisley Consulting's Risk Navigator.

Compliancy difficulties that Bandag faced included:

- The requirement of a quick solution implementation as deadlines approached
- Integration for international companies
- A need for future changes

Bandag has found that this process provides an effective framework for compliance, testing internal controls, informing executives, and storing documentation. Johnson also chose Paisley Consulting in order to facilitate quick implementation.

One of the greatest benefits that Bandag has found is that Risk Navigator, as a web-based system, allows access for employees and external auditors, regardless of their location anywhere in the world. The system allows all persons to manage their controls and provides them with a list of people to whom the updates should be forwarded.

In The Real World (continued)

Bandag also found that by writing risks in English and controls in the local language of their international locations, it was able to have users understand and own the controls, providing direct sign-off.

Finally, Johnson and his team were able to quickly customize the product manually, which allowed them to design each control for each business unit. This strategy is also enabling Bandag to add business units.

[a] Kathleen Ohlson, "Case Study: Bandag, a Tire Company, Treads Softly on SOX Compliance," *AdtMag* (June 2005).

Disclaimer: This information is in no way meant to be an endorsement or otherwise of any products, services, or companies mentioned.

As a result of their review, the PCAOB determined that while the audits are valuable, their process is in need of revision. To this end, the changes involve:

- *Creating greater focus within the audit process.* By instructing auditors to employ a top-down approach, the PCAOB is able to make the auditing process more efficient and better focused on relevant controls, thereby improving time and cost management for compliant companies.

  The new standard also directs auditors to focus on risk assessment at each significant decision point in order to direct them toward the significant controls and to help determine the amount of evidence required to certify that a control is effective.

  Finally, the new standard refines the requirements of a material or significant deficiency not only to make the terms more clear, but also to allow more room for auditors to use their judgment.

Doing so enables auditors to have greater control in determining which controls are risk related.

- *Eliminating unnecessary procedures.* Another way in which the process is streamlined and costs are made more manageable is through the elimination of unnecessary procedures. Procedures deemed superfluous are those that evaluate control evaluation processes, require extensive evaluation of low-risk controls by auditors, or evaluate redundant processes that have already been completed at other sites or by other parties.

  Auditors previously were required to evaluate the process management used to evaluate internal controls. Under the new standards, auditors need only to understand management's process and can forgo evaluating it as long as the company's reporting systems provide sufficient information for auditors to release their opinion on the efficacy of the controls.

  Additionally, auditors are now able to use their judgment to determine which controls are linked to material risks and which can be tested with less frequency. If auditors have evidence that the control was previously tested effective and that no changes have occurred that would compromise that efficacy, then they can test the control only as needed.

  In keeping with the risk-based approach, auditors are now able to use their judgment and risk assessment to determine which locations of a multilocation company need to be included in the audit. Similarly, both financial statement audits and integrated audits will now be able to include some externally obtained information and data, given that the documentation can be judged relevant and accurate.

- *Simplifying overall requirements.* A simplification of AS No. 2 compliance requirements not only ensures that companies and auditors will have an easier time in their efforts, but also that the results and subsequent level of control will be improved.

  The PCAOB has never intended that compliance be based on a laundry list of checks and tasks. Instead, by simplifying the requirements, the PCAOB is able to return the focus to the key principles of SOX—integrity, accountability, and accuracy—which ensures that those principles do not get lost in compliance efforts and enables companies to adapt their efforts to suit their unique circumstances.

The new standard is meant to address several concerns associated with SOX, including:

- *Improving the efficiency of the audits by focusing only on important internal controls.* The new standard will also increase the emphasis on risk assessment to further encourage a cost-effective process.
- *Reducing difficulties in defining ambiguous terms*, such as "material weakness" and "strong indicator," by clarifying their definitions.
- *Improving efficiency by removing unnecessary tasks*, such as evaluating the management's process. It will also permit the consideration of information from previous audits and remove the barriers from using information from outside sources.

TIPS AND TECHNIQUES

Steps of an Internal Control Audit

Part of SOX compliance includes conducting internal control audits to verify their efficacy. Six steps toward the implementation of an internal control audit are:

1. Plan the audit.
2. Evaluate management's assessment process.
3. Discover and research internal controls.
4. Test and evaluate efficacy of internal control design.
5. Test and evaluate efficacy of internal control operations.
6. Evaluate sufficiency of company's internal control testing.

Based on the results of these steps, the auditor formulates an opinion regarding the internal controls efficiency with regard to financial reporting. The auditor then issues a report of findings and an opinion to the audit committee and company management.

- *Alleviating the burden on small companies* by providing the auditor with instructions to scale the audit to match the company's size and complexity.
- *Simplifying the requirements and paperwork involved* by broadening details and improving audit readability.

Conclusion

Many companies have found that several challenges presented by SOX mitigate their compliance efforts. One of the biggest challenges lies in the fact that neither the Act nor the auditor provides much guidance in how to actually achieve compliance.

Although each company's efforts will reflect its unique circumstances, SOX compliance strategies center on a framework that includes:

- Evaluating risks and establishing a plan
- Creating a control framework
- Designing specific controls
- Documenting control activity
- Evaluating control design
- Testing control effectiveness

Companies and consultants alike have found that the development of a SOX compliance strategy is a process of continual problem solving and an exercise in patience as well as organization.

This chapter focused on some compliance issues that companies regularly face. Recognizing these issues illustrates that further development is still required on the road to creating efficient compliance strategies.

Summary

- SOX compliance is not an easy process; many challenges must be overcome.
- Part of SOX compliance is documenting internal controls, including the tone at the top.

- Compliance strategies will take many forms depending on the nature of the company.
- The PCAOB Audit Standard No. 2 is an evolving standard that creates guidelines for executives' and auditors' control evaluation responsibilities.

Note

1. More information regarding the PCAOB Audit Standard No. 2 can be found at www.pcaobus.org/Standards/Standards_and_Related_Rules/Auditing_Standard_No.2.aspx.

CHAPTER 5

Industry Frameworks

After reading this chapter, you will be able to:

- Understand the importance of the Committee of Sponsoring Organizations (COSO) and its internal control framework.
- Understand the importance of the Control Objectives for Information and Related Technology (COBIT), its six components, and its four domains.

Introduction

The Sarbanes-Oxley Act (SOX) mandates the establishment of internal controls to protect the interests of shareholders but does not provide much guidance as to how companies are to establish these measures. One of the first steps that a company must take toward SOX compliance is to establish a suitable framework that will enable evaluation of its internal controls. This framework will also facilitate assessment of agreement between the company executive and the external auditor.

In terms of general frameworks for compliance, the Committee of Sponsoring Organizations (COSO) internal control framework is the one most commonly used by companies. Similarly, COBIT is the most popular internal information technology (IT) control framework for companies seeking SOX compliance.

Committee of Sponsoring Organizations

Established in October 1985, the Treadway Commission is a U.S. private-sector initiative whose primary objective has been to offer solutions to reduce the incidence of fraudulent financial reporting. Its establishment was a reaction to the enactment of the 1977 Foreign Corrupt Practices Act (FCPA) and other financial law reforms designed to combat fraudulent corporate political campaign finance practices.

After filing its initial report in 1987, which called for a concerted effort to develop guidance on internal controls, the Treadway Commission established the Committee of Sponsoring Organizations whose guidelines are highly respected standards in corporate governance and internal controls.

Since the inception of SOX, these guidelines have become the most commonly employed framework for SOX Section 404 compliance and have received specific endorsement by the Securities and Exchange Commission (SEC).

Associations

Five major professional associations sponsor COSO:

1. American Institute of Certified Public Accountants (AICPA)
2. American Accounting Association (AAA)
3. Financial Executives Institute (FEI, now called the Financial Executives International)
4. Institute of Internal Auditors (IIA)
5. Institute of Management Accountants (IMA)

Internal Control Philosophies of COSO

The guidelines that COSO (www.coso.org) puts forth are widely accepted as best standards for corporate governance and SOX compliance. These guidelines center on COSO's internal control philosophies.

First, creating and sustaining internal control must be viewed as an ongoing process. It cannot be treated as a one-time objective because it is a part of a progression toward eliminating the release of fraudulent information.

Second, in order to maintain internal controls effectively, the efforts cannot end with the creation of policy manuals and forms, but must also focus on the mind-set of those people involved at all levels of the organization.

Third, the limitations of internal control efforts must be understood. Even the most effective internal control can provide only a reasonable level of assurance, and must therefore always be handled speculatively.

By adopting and implementing these philosophies into their companies, publicly traded organizations will be better equipped to meet the demands of SOX compliance.

Internal Control Framework

Initially the COSO Internal Control Framework contained five components required to achieve effective internal control. After the inception of SOX, COSO published *Enterprise Risk Management: Integrated Framework,*[1] which serves to elaborate and expand on those five initial components to better adapt them to the post-SOX world. The eight components discussed in the *Integrated Framework* include:

1. *Internal environment.* To evaluate their internal environment, the company must engage in planning and assessment of its organizational format and other processes. This includes an evaluation of the manner in which decisions are made and policies are established. It also includes the process of cataloging the ways in which authority and responsibility are assigned.
2. *Objective setting.* In the processes of objective setting, the company clearly identifies the goals and objectives to be achieved through the compliance process.
3. *Event identification.* Here the company isolates the processes that are linked to the accuracy of the financial reports.
4. *Risk assessment.* Risk assessment involves pinpointing those processes that pose threats to the accuracy and integrity of the financial reports. It also includes an evaluation ofhow the processes

are preformed and how this specifically relates to their impact on the financial reports.

5. *Risk response.* This step involves developing clear intentions to minimize or eliminate those exploitable processes.
6. *Control activities.* This step involves designing and implementing controls to meet the objectives developed through the risk response stage. These controls must be specifically tailored to mitigate the risks that have been identified and should fit the intentions created in the risk response stage.
7. *Information and communication.* Here the company establishes processes for creating and storage of all documentation regarding the control developments and their assessments. It also establishes processes to direct communication among relevant parties as to important occurrences.
8. *Monitoring.* This stage includes testing, monitoring, and maintaining controls to ensure that they remain effective. The stage also serves to identify new or previously unrecognized risks.

Control Objectives for Informational and Related Technology

The IT Governance Institute (ITGI) is responsible for the issuance of the COBIT standards. Although COBIT guidelines were established pre-SOX in 1996, they have since become a widely accepted SOX compliance framework.[2] In fact, COBIT is considered the most commonly used framework for information technology (IT) controls. To better meet the needs of the post-SOX world, ISACA has released *IT Control Objectives for Sarbanes-Oxley.*

Six Components of COBIT

Applying the COBIT framework requires an understanding of these six components:

1. *Executive Summary.* This section includes understanding and identifying those concepts and principles essential to the IT system.
2. *Framework.* This section formulates the IT process model's organization into four domains (outlined in the next section):

   Plan and organize
   Acquire and implement
   Deliver and support
   Monitor and evaluate

3. *Control Objective.* This section identifies the aim of the control as specifically linked to the IT risk areas that it is seeking to eliminate.
4. *Control Practices.* This section identifies the best practices and describes requirements for specific IT controls to be implemented.
5. *Management Guidelines.* This section provides the informational links between both the business and IT objectives.
6. *Audit Guidelines.* This section offers evaluation strategies to assess compliance. These strategies include:

   Document financial reporting internal controls
   Test and evaluate internal controls.
   Support external audits
   Document compliance efforts
   Report deficiencies

Four COBIT Domains

COBIT defines four domains, which serve as a means to logically segregate our analysis of IT governance within the organization. Employing COBIT requires moving through these four domains (see Exhibit 5.1).

EXHIBIT 5.1

Employing the COBIT Framework, or One that is Similar, Requires Moving Through the Four COBIT Domains.

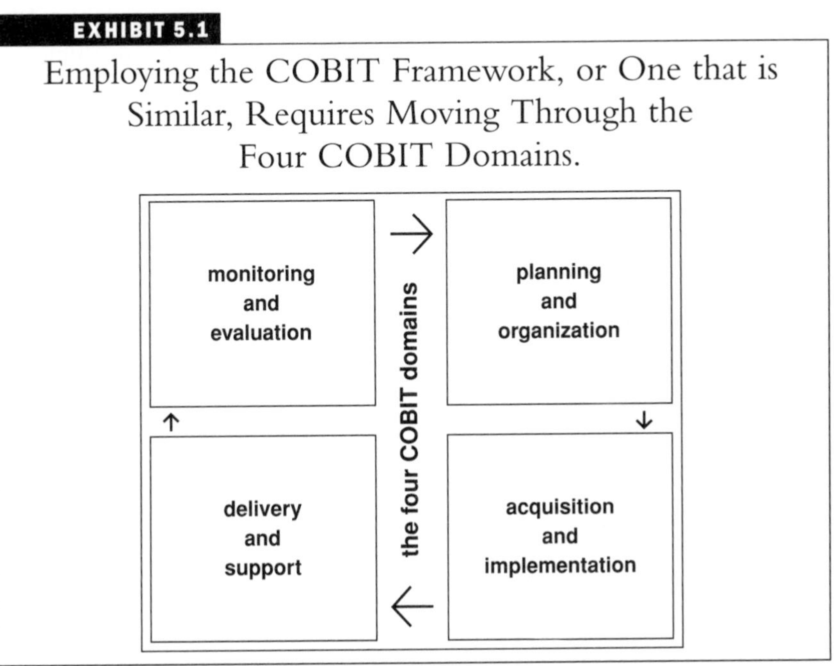

1. *Planning and Organization.* This section involves establishing effective and strategic IT plans that support not only SOX compliance but also business-related goals. Related tasks include:

   - Form channels of communication among IT management, business process owners, and relevant executives.
   - Develop plans for aligning business and IT objectives.

- Define information controls to facilitate and support the quality and integrity of financial disclosure information.
- Define the data classification system and assign security levels.

2. *Acquisition and Implementation.* Depending on how the plan is developed, new applications and other resources may be required. Following acquisition, implementation occurs, which includes testing, altering, and maintaining systems. Related tasks include:
   - Acquire required software and technology.
   - Monitor software installation and maintenance in accordance with the organization's predetermined requirements, including data security strategies.
3. *Delivery and Support.* After implementation, the system is evaluated to ensure that it is meeting continuing expectations and that it is serviced through Service-Level Agreement (SLA) support. Related tasks include:
   - Acquire contact with outsourced vendors and qualify their skills and abilities.
   - Establish performance expectations for SLAs.
   - Ensure that risks, security controls, and procedures for information systems are clearly addressed in contracts.
   - Establish a regular schedule for security and processing integrity review.
4. *Monitoring and Evaluation.* The system establishes pars against which the organization can evaluate its performance. This provides an excellent opportunity for proactive management. Related tasks include:

- Evaluate service deliveries of IT programs and improve on shortfalls.

IN THE REAL WORLD

Six Sigma

Six Sigma is a method for striving for near perfection. It is a data-driven approach for identifying and eliminating defects. There are two submethodologies:

1. Six Sigma DMAIC is an improvement system to be implemented after identifying inadequacies in current processes. The steps of this system are Define, Measure, Analyze, Improve, Control (DMAIC).
2. Six Sigma DMADV is an improvement system for the development of new processes or complete overhaul of current processes. The steps of this system are Define, Measure, Analyze, Design, Verify (DMADV).

A strong benefit of this framework is the fact that it is applicable for any process and has been proven effective in compliance strategies for SOX.

- Monitor internal control effectiveness through internal assessments or independent audits.

Conclusion

Establishing an effective system of controls first requires the development of an internal control standard. Although several such standards exist, the SEC recommends the use of COSO or one very similar to it.

Irrespective of which system a company opts for, it should include these areas of guidance:

- Instructions as to how to assess the current environment, develop compliance committees, and establish systems for documentation.
- Guidance for determining which risks and controls are related to material effects in data and documents.
- Systematic approaches for establishing documentation controls and creating systems of communication within the company and with relevant, external parties.
- Clear monitoring and testing guidance that includes instruction on how to establish, evaluate, document, and report on monitoring and testing processes.

SOX is meant to protect the rights of the shareholders. In order to do so, the establishment and evaluation of internal controls, both IT and otherwise, is a key component.

Summary

- COSO is recommend by the SEC and is the most popular framework employed by companies.
- COBIT is the most popular framework designed specifically for internal IT controls.

Notes

1. Committee of Sponsoring Organizations of the Treadway Commission, *COSO Enterprise Risk Management—Integrated Framework* (AICPA, 2004).
2. Additional information on COBIT can be found at www.isaca.org/cobit.

CHAPTER 6

Achieving Sustainable Compliance

After reading this chapter, you will be able to:

- Understand the costs associated with Sarbanes-Oxley Act (SOX) compliance.
- Understand factors that have contributed to high costs in the past and those that will decrease costs in the future.
- Understand the Public Company Accounting Oversight Board (PCAOB) and its recommendations to help companies minimize compliance costs.
- Understand technology's contribution to sustainable compliance.

Introduction

The majority of corporate backlash against the Sarbanes-Oxley Act (SOX) stems from the high costs associated with implementing its requirements around internal controls. Many companies discovered that they had to make significant changes to, or even completely replace, existing systems for document management, access to financial data, and long-term information storage.

Cost of Compliance

The overall cost of SOX compliance has been quite large, and compliance with Section 404 has been identified as carrying the most significant costs. In fact, according to a survey of 217 companies with revenues exceeding $5 billion that was conducted by Financial Executives International (FEI), the average cost of Section 404 compliance in the first year was $4.36 million.[1] Additional reports have placed estimates of first-year compliance even higher. The Big Four accounting firms commissioned a report stating that of 90 large companies, the average cost was $7.8 million.[2] AMR Research has estimated that collectively approximately $6 billion per year is being spent on SOX compliance when all related costs, including increased audit fees, were considered.[3]

IN THE REAL WORLD

Compliance Costs

Through its September 2005 survey titled "Emerging Trends in Internal Controls: Fourth Survey and Industry Insights," Ernst & Young established and compiled these data:

In The Real World (continued)

- Of the surveyed companies with annual revenues in excess of $20 billion, 85% invested over $10 million to achieve year-one Section 404 compliance.
- Of those same companies, 25% tested between 10,000 and 50,000 controls.

Perhaps the most telling conclusion drawn from this survey is that there is a direct correlation between the quantity of tested controls and the cost of compliance. As a result, it is advisable that companies employ a top-down approach and test only those controls that are related to high-risk accounts and services.

Ernst & Young, "Emerging Trends in Internal Controls: Fourth Survey and Industrial Insights," 2005.

The actual costs associated with SOX compliance vary depending on the unique circumstances of the company. Factors that will affect cost include the size of the company, how central the company's organization is, the sophistication of the controls already in place, and whether the company initiated its compliance efforts early or waited.

Tips and Techniques

Areas of Spending Related to SOX Compliance

As companies enter into initial or continuing SOX compliance efforts, they need to understand the areas in which they will be required to divert resources. Recognizing these costs early in

Tips and Techniques (continued)

the planning of a strategy will allow for greater management and more opportunity to control costs.

- *Staffing*
  - *Additional hours of current staff*. Several companies found that throughout their first-year compliance efforts, they were required to divert staff attention from regular duties and increase working hours wherever possible to balance compliance with business.
  - *Costs associated hiring additional staff*. Due to a recent past of postbubble downsizing, several companies discovered that they simply lacked the number of employees required to meet their compliance needs. The costs associated with hiring new staff include recruiting and training costs as well as additional wages or salaries.
  - *Costs associated with training new and existing staff regarding compliance required changes*. In order to facilitate effective compliance, all staff members should understand not only the compliance efforts and their importance, but also the ethical policies of the company.
- *Consulting fees for various services*. There are several times throughout SOX compliance efforts when it is necessary to hire consultants. The bulk of consulting fees will be allocated to the accounting firms.
- *Technology*. Costs include: purchasing of software and new technology, installation, costs associated with training staff, and maintenance.

Many companies have argued that SOX compliance requires an unreasonable commitment of their resources, both in terms of personnel and finances. Several companies have had to delay expansions, seek loans, and otherwise divert funds to increase their SOX budgets, efforts that they argue create undue financial burden.

Factors Relating to High Initial Cost

One of the greatest factors for the high initial costs during the initial years of compliance is inadequate maintenance of former controls. The requirements put forth by SOX are not outlandish, but those companies that did not have a system of controls already in place or did not maintain their system of controls struggled to make up for lost time.

Another factor that created inflated costs of compliance was the initial misunderstanding of the breadth of Section 404. When first introduced to this section, companies and accounting firms underestimated the depth to which they would have to go. As a result, their initial plans and control developments were insufficient, requiring them to redo a great deal of work.

Additionally, many companies found that they did not plan adequately for the financial or time costs for required control remediation. They failed to recognize that several controls would have to be tested, redeveloped, and retested. Further compounding these costs for many was the fact that their system documentation and storage processes had to be either updated or established for the first time.

Finally, all costs associated with SOX compliance were exacerbated by the lack of staff created over years of downsizing. As a result of the personnel shortages, many companies were forced to rely heavily on outsourcing. These costs rose even higher given the nature of the market at the time.

Because all companies were rushing to meet the compliance deadlines, the service providers on which they relied were unable to meet the demand. As a result, the cost of those services increased exponentially, in some cases almost doubling. In fact, the fees for external audits of internal controls increased by 40% between January and July 2004.[4]

CEO/CFO Responsibilities

The chief executive and chief financial officers:

- Hold responsibility for establishing systems and policies that protect the integrity of the company's financial documents
- Hold responsibility for the monitoring of those company controls that impact financial reporting
- Write a conclusion regarding the effectiveness of the financial reporting controls for the most recent fiscal year

Projected Decline of Costs

It is projected that the ongoing cost of maintaining compliance will decrease over the next few years. In fact, a report released by the Big Four accounting firms projected that most companies can expect year-two costs to decrease by almost 42%.[5]

TIPS AND TECHNIQUES

Employing a Top-Down Approach

The Public Company Accounting Oversight Board (PCAOB) strongly recommends that SOX compliance be achieved by employing a top-down approach as opposed to a bottom-up approach. Doing so will provide companies with a more efficient system and also greater control over the costs.

With the top-down approach, company-level controls are evaluated first. If they are strong and provide direct links and adequate

prevention of misstatements, the process-level testing can be minimized.

This system, unlike the bottom-up alternative, enables companies to determine risks and insufficiencies quickly as well as confirm the presence of adequate controls. It consists of three steps:

1. Conduct risk assessment at each decision point of the company-level controls.
2. Identify significant accounts.
3. Create controls and assessment strategies for only those accounts that are at risk of producing material impact on financial statements.

Several factors contribute to the easing of the financial pressure of compliance. One of the biggest contributors is the fact that after year-one compliance, companies will have established an effective framework and have built a strong foundation from which they can establish a maintenance program. This maintenance program will not require the same control developments, process replacements, and other activities involved in the initial establishment.

A second factor that will decrease costs is that the company will be more familiar with the control processes that will lead to greater systemization and less demand on its financial and personnel resources.

In addition, as the pressure created by the initial rush to achieve compliance has eased, external consultants and contractors will not experience as much demand on their services, and fees should return to a more reasonable level. It is unlikely, however, that fees will ever return to their pre-SOX point.

Finally, given the new Audit Standard No. 2 (AS No. 2), auditors are encouraged to adopt a top-down and risk-based assessment approach. This will limit the time spent on the evaluation of unnecessary controls and decrease the costs associated with the audits.

PCAOB Recommendations for Minimizing the Costs Associated with Section 404

The PCAOB recommends that companies employ a top-down, risk-based approach rather than a bottom-up assessment. According to the recommendation, doing so will not only save companies time and money, it will also provide a more tailored system of controls for better management of financial statement accuracy.

A top-down, risk-based approach focuses on company-level controls and significant accounts when developing the internal control framework. By adopting this strategy, companies will be more likely to target processes that have a significant impact on their financial statements.

A top-down approach also allows companies to better incorporate entity-level controls. While not directly related to changes in figures on the financial records sheet, such controls do play a significant role in the overall compliance effort.

TIPS AND TECHNIQUES

Understanding Approach Types

- *Top-down.* This approach is based on the principle that not all accounts, transactions, or risks are equally important.

  In employing this approach, companies assess the item's significance, its risk level, and the efficacy of controls.
- *Bottom-up.* This approach implements and tests controls on all accounts and systems, irrespective of their contribution to financial risk. Those companies that have employed this approach have found it to be largely inefficient and highly expensive.
- *Risk-based.* Preventive controls proactively attempt to prevent unauthorized or undesirable acts from happening
- *Discovery-based.* Detective controls are designed to detect unauthorized acts after they have occurred.

Technology and Sustainable Compliance

Software and other technological advancements may enable companies to reduce their SOX compliance costs by limiting the scope of controls and improving the efficiency of testing.

In the first years after SOX's enactment, companies were encouraged to focus their control development efforts on those areas that have demonstrated exposure. This is sound advice; unfortunately, many companies have not established clear criteria on which to base the determination of risk. This has meant that internal financial controls have been tested for SOX compliance based largely on speculation. As a result, companies have wasted time and resources by testing irrelevant processes and have compromised their compliance efforts by missing important risks.

New software with scoping features allows companies to assess whether accounts are within the scope of SOX before dedicating themselves to developing control processes. Accurately identifying critical accounts and processes will eliminate the occurrence of irrelevant testing and streamline compliance efforts.

IN THE REAL WORLD

SOX and Technological Advancement

One unanticipated benefit of SOX has been its impact on software and technology advancements. By creating a greater demand for software solutions related to internal controls and risk assessment, SOX has fostered substantial improvements and developments in information technology. Not only will these advances allow for greater risk control, they will also facilitate the abilities of companies to achieve and maintain SOX compliance in a financially accessible manner.

The new software employs this scoping feature through an assessment of potential impact that any given account can have on the balance sheet. If the impact is not of material importance, then the company can eliminate it from those tested for internal controls. By limiting testing to only those accounts within the scope of SOX, these programs can help companies streamline their efforts, thereby limiting expenses.

Sustainable Compliance Strategies

Align Annual and Quarterly Reporting

Three strategies are available to maximize efficiency and meet Section 302's quarterly report requirements and Section 404's annual report requirements. The strategy that the company chooses should accurately reflect the most cost-effective method of identifying material changes over internal financial reporting controls.

1. *Continual testing*. Companies that conduct tests throughout the year have time for remediation and retesting while meeting Sections 302 and 304 requirements.
2. *Quarterly testing*. Other companies conduct quarterly tests on high-risk controls and supplement these data with self-assessments for other processes.
3. *Self-assessment*. A final alternative is to conduct quarterly reporting based only on self-assessment, meaning that no testing is conducted.

When selecting a strategy, the company will have to determine whether any changes have occurred since the last report that would create the potential for a different result. Companies therefore need to evaluate whether sufficient evidence exists to guarantee that the control is still as effective as it was at the previous testing.

Employ a Controls Rationalization for Testing

By conducting a thorough assessment of all company activities, it should be possible to determine which are most susceptible to contributing to misrepresentation in financial reports through error or fraud. This information can then allow for the creation of a testing hierarchy whereby the controls of high-risk activities can be tested more frequently and those of less significant ones can be tested intermittently or even not at all.

Conclusion

The price tag associated with SOX compliance, particularly with efforts related to Sections 302 and 404, have posed a financial challenge for a number of companies. Although most saw at least partial reductions in year two and beyond, efforts are still being made to further reduce costs and promote sustainable compliance.

Summary

- SOX compliance is an expensive endeavor, in many cases costing around $10 million annually.
- In many situations, high costs can be at least partially attributed to inadequate planning and poor maintenance of controls in previous years.
- The PCAOB recommends a top-down, risk-based approach to help contain costs and provide the most efficient results.
- Technological advancements have helped contain costs and are continuing to improve efficiencies.

Notes

1. Available through www.fei.org.
2. Robert E. Litan, "Sarbanes-Oxley Section 404 Costs and Implementation Issues," *CRA International*, www.s-oxinternalcontrolinfo.com/pdfs/CRA_III.pdf. December 8, 2005.
3. www.amrresearch.com.
4. Financial Executives International, "FEI Special Survey on Sarbanes-Oxley Section 404 Implementation," July, 2004. www.fei.com.
5. CRA International, "Sarbanes-Oxley Section 404 Costs and Implementation Issues: Spring 2006 Survey Update" Washington, 2006.

CHAPTER 7

Technology Solutions

After reading this chapter, you will be able to:

- Understand the value of information technology (IT) in SOX compliance.
- Understand the process for successful implementation of IT controls.
- Understand the concept of subcertification and when is it required.
- Understand various security best practices, including the IT Infrastructure Library (ITIL), the National Institute of Standards and Technology (NIST), and the International Organization for Standardization and the International Electrotechnical Commission (ISO/IEC) 17799 Framework.
- Understand Extensible Business Reporting Language (XBRL) and its future implications.

- Understand the uses of enterprise resource planning (ERP) software.

Introduction

The Sarbanes-Oxley Act (SOX) makes little mention of technology itself, but it does have a significant and direct impact on the information technology (IT) department of companies.

SOX compliance is largely concerned with financial reporting, and financial reporting is intricately related to a company's IT environment. This is a direct result of the fact that most organizations operate their financial reporting processes through their IT systems.

SOX Sections 302 and 404 require that financial information be reported accurately, completely, and in a timely fashion. The efficacy with which this is done is depends significantly on IT controls. When an IT control is working effectively, it will prevent the risk of fraudulent reporting and typically will ensure that errors are caught early in the cycle.

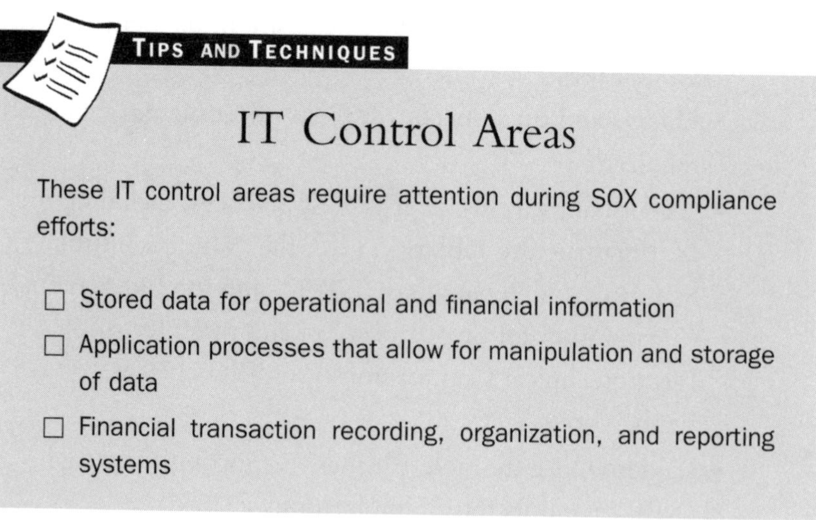

TIPS AND TECHNIQUES

IT Control Areas

These IT control areas require attention during SOX compliance efforts:

- ☐ Stored data for operational and financial information
- ☐ Application processes that allow for manipulation and storage of data
- ☐ Financial transaction recording, organization, and reporting systems

Tips and Techniques (continued)

- ☐ Executive and administrative activities
- ☐ Board activities

It is clear that when the information collected within the IT environment is unreliable, the integrity of the company's financial reporting systems is severely compromised. This is why a company's IT environment can have such an important impact on its ability to comply with SOX.

Despite its importance, IT control management often is overlooked by companies that focus all their resources on business process controls. Many companies fear the cost of revamping their systems; others simply do not know where to start. Compounding this issue, SOX provides no information regarding the nature of IT controls that have to be adopted in order to achieve SOX compliance.

In the Real World

Outsourcing Dilemma

Companies and corporations often outsource their IT requirements to help control costs. Since the inception of SOX, however, IT outsourcing has become a bit more involved. Since SOX compliance requires that management be accountable and able to attest to internal control systems, the creation of these systems can no longer be outsourced as easily.

One of the most important considerations is that chief executive officers (CEOs) and chief financial officers (CFOs) understand that sourcing these services to providers outside of the company does not diminish or eliminate their own responsibility for the control's efficacy.

In The Real World (continued)

The most common solution is for the outsourced company to obtain Statement on Auditing Standards No. 70 (SAS 70), which serves as an assurance that the company is meeting SOX compliance requirements. Without a SAS 70, each company would have to visit its outsourcing organizations and conduct audits of the internal controls. The SAS 70 is a single verification that proves to be more cost effective and efficient, while serving the same purpose.

IT Components Relevant to SOX Compliance

Companies that are required to comply with SOX have found (or should find) that their IT divisions are integrally involved in the process. The right software and processes can make control testing and monitoring a much simpler and more efficient task. Although SOX makes little direct mention of IT in its pages, it does imply the necessity of IT processes through several of its requirements.

IT systems and process improvements are required to ensure that these SOX requirements are met:

- Accelerated reporting
- Internal controls
- Certification requirements
- Record keeping
- Communications

Accelerated Reporting Requirements

SOX requires that investors and other relevant parties receive financial reporting information in a timely manner. This requirement demands that the IT division establish systems that will assemble data in a centralized data repository. This requirement also means that relevant information should be sent quickly to executive officers for evaluation before the public release.

Tips and Techniques

Establishing an Access Control Model

One of the most important steps in creating effective IT controls is establishing security measures over which company members have access to data (see Exhibit 7.1).

1. *Create a list of users who are able to directly access, contribute, and create information for financial statements.* This step requires a complete list of company members who currently have the power to obtain, modify, or establish documents and data pertaining to financial disclosure.
2. *Establish a security hierarchy of documents and access.* By establishing a comprehensive list of which documents are high security and which are low, the company will be able to manage access to those documents that could directly impact SOX compliance.
3. *Limit document access to those employees with proper security clearance.* After establishing the security level of each document, company members also need to be organized in a similar hierarchy of which ones require which level of access. Essentially, the higher the sensitivity of the document, the higher the security clearance required to access it.
4. *Create a unique access service directory for those who require such access.* A unique access service directory establishes a one-stop login for all employees, but directs their activities

TIPS AND TECHNIQUES (CONTINUED)

only to those documents and processes for which they have received security clearance. For example, while a CEO password may grant the ability to modify a document, an entry-level employee would have "read-only" access or perhaps no access at all.

EXHIBIT 7.1

Establishing an Access Control Model Allows Companies to Regulate Which Employees are Able to Use Files Based on Their Security Clearance.

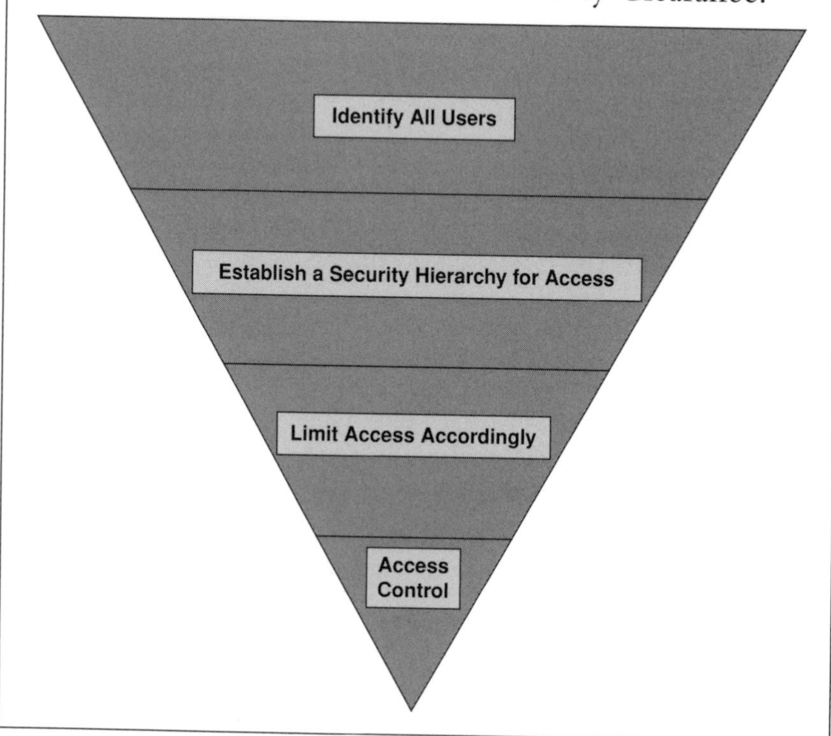

Accelerated reporting requirements are directly related to the Securities and Exchange Commission (SEC) Form 8-K that companies must file with every event that could create a material impact on their financial information.

Internal Controls

One of the primary objectives of SOX is to ensure that companies secure the integrity and accuracy of their financial records and reports.

This is achieved by establishing controls at every potential vulnerability point along the chain. These controls need to be monitored and tested regularly in order to achieve compliance.

A company's IT division serves an integral role in the establishment, monitoring, and testing of internal controls. Without adequate software and technology, the processes related to internal controls would be lengthy and costly.

One aspect of internal control establishment is the development of an access control system. As a company establishes its internal controls for SOX compliance, the IT division will be involved in establishing processes that provide limited access to sensitive documents.

The IT division will also be responsible for establishing systems by which top management can implement and monitor controls and processes. This will include tracking the flow of documentation and financial information.

Certification Requirement

SOX requires that company CEOs and CFOs certify that internal controls have been developed and tested to ensure the accuracy of the company's financial reports and other related documents.

In order to assist the CEO and CFO in their certification requirements, the IT systems of a company must include these considerations:

- Systems to accurately and effectively capture data and documentation that will be relevant to financial reports
- Systems of security to guarantee the safety and privacy of information as it travels within the company's networks
- Centralized storage system to securely accumulate and protect all important data and documentation
- Systems to control access and provide hierarchical security clearance for accessing stored data and documentation
- Systems for regular document destruction based on company policies

Record Keeping

SOX requires that auditors maintain relevant records for seven years, and it is recommended that companies do the same. This means that IT must be involved in the establishment of a system for managing and maintaining the important documents. The record-keeping system also needs to include a system whereby unnecessary documents are disposed of on a scheduled basis.

Communications

SOX Section 806 requires that the privacy of whistle-blowers be protected in order to foster the reporting of illegal and other unwanted behaviors. IT systems can help facilitate anonymous communication systems between employees and the internal audit committee to ensure compliance with this section. IT will also be involved in establishing systems used in investigating such reports as well as the secure storage of all related documents.

IN THE REAL WORLD

Health Insurance Portability and Accountability Act

The Health Insurance Portability and Accountability Act (HIPAA) requires that companies create systems to protect the privacy and security of documents related to their employees' health insurance. This Act is an extension of related medical privacy acts that serve to ensure that the medical history and files of citizens cannot be viewed by unauthorized parties.

Both SOX and HIPAA require the establishments of processes that ensure secure information storage including:

- ☐ Controlled access to local data
- ☐ Maintenance of critical data backups
- ☐ Controlled access to backup data

Compliance with both acts includes:

- ☐ Password protection
- ☐ Automatic user lockouts
- ☐ Security hierarchies for access

Because of their similar requirements, cost-effective compliance efforts can seek to meet the mandates of both acts using the same process controls.

Relevant SOX Sections for IT

Compliance with SOX Section 302 requires the development of internal controls. Within the company's IT environment, these controls need to ensure that financial reports and statements are prepared using generally accepted accounting principles (GAAP). In addition, Section 302 also requires the establishment and maintenance of internal controls to facilitate management and documentation.

Compliance with SOX Section 404 mandates the implementation of data protection systems to safeguard against the possibility of misrepresentation in annual reports. It also requires that companies establish systems to ensure that data are protected from destruction, loss, unauthorized alteration, and other misuse.

TIPS AND TECHNIQUES

Building an IT Road Map

Technology is a rapidly changing field, and companies often find it difficult to keep up with new innovations. Staying abreast of the developments of new software and tools can be vital to remaining competitive with their industry. Now, with SOX on the forefront of the minds of all public companies, new technologies can help develop more efficient processes and enhanced security of internal controls.

All new technology needs to be evaluated in terms of the impact that it will have on compliance efforts. It should also be evaluated in terms of the benefits it offers toward the company's business interests.

Tips and Techniques (continued)

In order to ensure that technological advancements and acquisitions will improve the company's performance and also conform to the compliance plan, it is recommended that companies establish an IT road map for guidance.

To develop a road map, a company must create a dialog between the IT divisions and the operating personnel. This dialog will ensure that those involved in acquiring and establishing new technologies have the information and input required. Creating the road map as a joint, interdivision effort will also reflect the company's commitment to integrating its compliance efforts at all levels and within all divisions. The road map should reflect the company's current IT position, the changes that must be undertaken for SOX compliance, and any upgrades that are hoped for in the future.

After creating a road map, it is vital that the company review and update it regularly to reflect changes to business interests as well as technological advancements.

Steps for Successful Implementation of IT Controls

The steps for implementing effective IT controls include:

- *Risk assessment.* The first step to control implementation is the assessment of high-risk areas that could be exploited, thereby influencing financial reports. Risk assessment looks for any vulnerable transactions where information could be mistaken or falsified. To this end, IT management must evaluate the current systems, including the accuracy of all relevant documentation.

- *Monitoring.* The processes for auditing must be developed to monitor high-risk IT areas. In addition, tests must be created to facilitate internal audits of the controls and their effectiveness. These internal audits should be conducted by IT personnel, although their efforts will be complemented by external audits. It is up to the company how frequently these tests are completed, but for high-risk processes they should be done on a regular, frequent basis.
- *Communication.* Open and frequent communication channels must be established to ensure that IT management receives accurate and timely information. Too often in companies, divisions are compartmentalized and isolated from the events in other areas.

TIPS AND TECHNIQUES

Establishing Access Control: Challenges and Solutions

SOX requires that companies establish controls to protect the accuracy of financial documents. This is a key area in which the IT division will become involved in the compliance effort.

One of the biggest components of IT controls is ensuring that data and information can be accessed and altered only by appropriate persons. In order to control access to SOX-related files, a company must:

- ☐ *Limit access to sensitive documents.* The first goal needs to be limit access to those documents that can have a material impact on the accuracy of the financial reports. By controlling

Tips and Techniques (continued)

who views and edits the relevant information, the company will have greater control and also clearer records.

The solution is that the company establishes a process for login security. This means that all employees with access to documents are cataloged and entered in the system.

- ☐ *Minimize risks associated with passwords.* Login security is effective only when the security wall cannot be broken. Employees sharing passwords or selecting easily discovered ones is a serious threat to document security.

  The solution is to employ a process that allows for the creation of strict password selection parameters and expiry dates. Even better, companies can opt for the implementation of a non–password-based system including biometric, smart-card, or token authorization.

- ☐ *Establish multilevel security with users at distinct levels.* Part of controlling who views and edits sensitive documents is determining which positions within the company require such privileges. After all company members (employees, customers, partners, etc.) have been cataloged and their current access levels have been determined, the next step is to modify the system so that the absolute fewest people are provided with access.

  The solution is to implement a system that demands reverification for access to processes at incremental security levels. For example, this means that some levels are provided with no access, view-only access, or full privileges, depending on their position in the company and the document in question.

- ☐ *Monitor and testing control efficacy.* Part of SOX compliance includes the monitoring and testing of controls on a continual basis to ensure their efficacy. Included here are the internal controls established by the IT department, especially those that are related to significant processes that pose potentially

Tips and Techniques (continued)

high risks. Depending on the company size, these tests can be monitored by one or several company members, but the information needs to be reported, accumulated, and stored in a systematic way.

The solution is to select or develop a system that offers confirmation of access and audits user activity, including access time, duration, activity, and any file modifications. A system such as this will provide a paper trail so that any problems with the controls can be traced back to their source.

- ☐ *Control design.* After identifying system risks, a framework of controls must be designed. The control design often includes a partial redesign of current controls and the development of new ones. Part of effective control design includes the creation of usage rules and audit trails for each system within the scope of SOX. Through this system, company members will have regulated access to specific systems and processes, and their activities will be monitored and documented for future reference.

When it comes to SOX compliance, IT plays such a vital role that this division must be kept abreast of changes, difficulties, and concerns that occur in other areas of the company. Without such information, it would be impossible for IT to react adequately to potential violations.

Part of the establishment of sufficient internal controls is the establishment of a reporting system whereby the right people receive the right information at the right time.

Subcertification

Although CEOs and CFOs must assume responsibility for IT internal controls, often they do not have the expertise or experience to personally evaluate the efficacy of those systems. As a result, many companies have adopted a policy of subcertification whereby the chief information officer (CIO) verifies that the controls are properly designed and effective.

TIPS AND TECHNIQUES

Subcertification and the CIO

CEOs and CFOs often do not have the education or background required to develop IT controls; still, under SOX, they are responsible for certification. To solve the difficulty that this presents, many companies have initiated a policy of subcertification.

After developing the internal controls, the CIO will certify the system's efficiency to assure the CEOs and CFOs that they are secure to do the same. Although not recognized by the PCAOB or SEC, subcertification is becoming a relatively common practice.

For the CIO not only to design controls but also to verify that they are effective requires that he or she have a complete understanding of SOX requirements and the company's plan for compliance.

In addition, the CIO must have expertise regarding IT internal controls that should include:

- ☐ Experience with internal controls
- ☐ The ability to identify, document, and test relevant application controls
- ☐ The ability to identify, document, and test relevant IT computer controls

This lack of direct knowledge violates the spirit of Section 404 because in truth the CEO and CFOs are not responsible for the controls, but rather are held responsible in spite of that fact. It is important that all members of the process understand this and are aware that in spite of a policy of subcertification, it the certifying corporate executive who is culpable for noncompliance.

In order to protect themselves and guarantee SOX compliance, public companies need to establish adequate documentation trails supporting control assessment. This means that when the CIO subcertifies the efficacy of the internal controls, the CEO and CFO must have a high degree of evidence to support the certification.

ISO/IEC 17799 Framework

As a combined effort of the International Organization for Standardization (ISO) and the International Electrotechnical Commission (IEC), the ISO/IEC 17999 Framework is formally called the Code of the Practice for Information Security Management. It has since been replaced by the ISO 27001 standard; however, the fundamental tenets are derived from ISO 17799 (also referred to as BS 7799 in the United Kingdom).

This document provides guidance for those who are responsible for information security management systems by outlining IT security controls and their implementation. Areas covered by ISO/IEC 17799 include:

- Physical security measures to limit access to IT instruments
- Personnel security to verify the credibility of employees to whom access is granted
- Development of access controls
- Organization and development of the organization's security
- Business continuity provisions

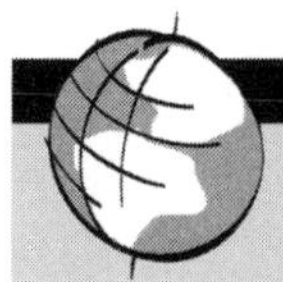

In the Real World

PDA Threat

Increased use of palm-held digital assistants (personal digital assistants, or PDAs) creates real security concerns when evaluating the integrity of a company's IT controls.

PDAs, cell phones, pocket PCs, and all other technologies that operate on wireless local area networks (LANs) create potential risks regarding information privacy and integrity. The use of these systems is ubiquitous in the corporate world, but companies need to ensure that their information can be neither stolen nor manipulated from a remote location.

This is just one of many security risks that require the establishment of an internal IT control.

Although it is generally agreed that compliance with ISO/IEC 17799 will greatly assist with SOX compliance, it may not be the most cost-effective method, as it throws its net fairly wide.

The ISO/IEC 17999 Framework does, however, provide a good deal of guidance for anyone looking to initiate a SOX compliance effort. The framework can be useful for CIOs who seek to complete airtight subcertification.

Security Best Practices

SOX does not expressly describe the compliance measures that companies should take toward the establishment of IT internal controls. In fact, as stated earlier, it makes little mention of information technology at all. This is because there is not necessarily a right or a wrong way to create the controls. SOX is simply concerned with the fact that the controls are created and that they are effective. In a sense, this means that IT is actually more governance related than regulation dictated.

As a result, many companies are looking toward the best security practices that have been established by other organizations. These companies have found that by meeting the requirements of these best practices, they are able to complete their SOX-related audits successfully.

IT Infrastructure Library

The IT Infrastructure Library (ITIL) system consists of an international series of documents that facilitate IT service management frameworks. It was developed by the U.K. Office of Government Commerce (OGC) with the intention that it would assist companies by allowing them to:

- Reduce costs
- Improve IT services
- Provide professional service delivery
- Heighten customer satisfaction
- Offer standards and guidance
- Improve skills and experience of employees
- Improve productivity

One of the benefits of this framework is that it contains guidelines rather than applications or platforms; this means that it is applicable to any company or organization.

IN THE REAL WORLD

CRM and SOX

Customer relationship management (CRM) is a software strategy adopted by companies that would like to improve efficiency and revenue by fostering customer loyalty. In its most ideal sense, this strategy combines information on each customer from every available data source and provides customer-facing employees the ability to make sales strategy decisions.

The impact that SOX compliance will have on CRM is a truly important and relevant concern, especially since many larger companies have invested millions of dollars to install and customize their CRM technology systems.

Although SOX does not directly create an impact on CRM strategies, as companies are required to adapt for SOX compliancy, it is likely that no aspect of the operation, including CRM, will go untouched.

Luckily, all indications point to CRM receiving nothing but benefits from SOX compliancy. These benefits are the result of several factors, including:

- *Improved training of workers who complete customer transactions.* This aids in accurate financial reporting and also presents customers with a higher caliber of company representative.
- *Stronger data integration and remediation of fragmented systems.* Establishing controls to ensure complete information integrity is essential to SOX compliance, and it also provides greater opportunity for CRM- related data collection.
- *Greater controls and procedures for customer transactions.* In addition to providing a strategy for risk management, these controls also improve the customer experience by creating a uniform experience regardless of the employee.

National Institute of Standards and Technology

The National Institute of Standards and Technology (NIST) is a nonregulatory federal agency that was established within the U.S. Commerce Department's Technology Administration in 1901. The overall goal of the NIST is to promote U.S. innovation and industrial competitiveness by enhancing economic security through the advancement of measurement science, standards, and technology.

NIST's Role-Based Access Control (RBAC) serves to restrict system access from unauthorized users. This system enables companies to track user information and activity including login times, durations, and file modifications.

TIPS AND TECHNIQUES

Selecting the Best Software for Now and the Future

When SOX was first introduced, companies were at a loss as to how to handle the required IT changes. Over time, however, new technology and software has been developed that can make compliance efforts more efficient and processes more secure.

The costs of new technology to assist in SOX compliance can be large. For this reason, it is vital to ensure that the software selected will not only facilitate initial compliance efforts, but also will provide assistance for compliance in the future.

To ensure that the selected software will meet ongoing needs, a company should:

- ☐ Evaluate the software's compatibility with the business and its SOX compliance efforts.

Tips and Techniques (continued)

- What is the cost of the technology, both initially and with ongoing support?
- What technology does the software use?
- What system will be required to maintain the software?
- Does the software function centrally or over the internet?

☐ Evaluate the software provider's security procedures and their compatibility with the company's SOX initiatives.

- Are there applications with limited access?
- How are users maintained?
- How are passwords created and maintained?
- Does the system have encrypted data transmission?
- What are the backup procedures?

☐ Evaluate the software's documentation capabilities.

- How are changes tracked?
- How is information communicated to the relevant parties?

☐ Evaluate the software's benefits aside from its contributions to the SOX compliance effort.

- What other features does the software offer?
- Are upgrades scheduled for the future?

By carefully evaluating their specific needs, both current and future, and then selecting the software that best suits those needs, companies will not only find greater compliance success, they will also be making strong strides toward keeping their compliance costs in check.

Software

SOX has created an entire new arena within the software market. In the years since its enactment, SOX-related technology has been developed to help companies achieve compliance more effectively and with a lower price tag.

Depending on the nature of the company, several software solutions are available to aid in its compliance efforts. There are monitoring tools that help companies keep track of electronic communications and transactions, and there are also compliance-in-a-box software packages that create centralized databases for controls and processes, but these are generally for smaller organizations.

Software tools have also been developed to help specific industries that have unique compliance circumstances because they fall under the jurisdiction of multiple regulatory boards. For example, companies in the healthcare industry that have to comply with SOX and other regulations benefit from software that will integrate their compliance requirements and help them meet all necessary regulations.

The most prevalent technologies that are receiving the most SOX-related attention are Extensible Business Reporting Language (XBRL) and enterprise resource planning (ERP).

XBRL

XBRL is an Extensible Markup Language (XML)-based standard for defining and exchanging financial information. Essentially, XBRL provides a viable option for companies to make the maintenance of a transparent system sustainable. XBRL soon will be available as a built-in application in financial software.

The value of XBRL is that it reduces duplication, improves information transparency, and facilitates real-time communication. This system also provides time and expense reductions by eliminating reentry requirements, thereby minimizing errors and simplifying reporting.

IN THE REAL WORLD

SEC's XBRL Voluntary Filing Program

Although widely anticipated and touted, XBRL has not been rolled out officially as part of SOX compliancy. It is, however, being mandated by certain countries. April 4, 2005 marked the start of the SEC's voluntary filing program on EDGAR using XBRL. This pilot program has been designed to assess XBRL technology for usability and benefits.

It is hoped that eventually XBRL will help publicly traded companies, accounting firms, the PCAOB, and the SEC in managing publicly traded efforts at SOX compliance, especially with Sections 302, 404, and 409.

Sections 302 and 404. Compliance with SOX Sections 302 and 404 can be facilitated through XBRL because this system allows for efficient maintenance and publishing of internal financial reporting controls. By eliminating the necessity of duplicate copies and limiting the human-based entry of data, XBRL helps strengthen security and limits error. Not only will this improve controls and help Sections 302 and 404 audits, it will also benefit the companies by establishing a more efficient system.

Section 409. SOX Section 409 requires timely reporting of specified events related to a company's financial position. When first discussed, this section created a great deal of fear in companies, which worried about the technical requirements that would be associated with the rapid responses required.

IN THE REAL WORLD

BlackRock Investment Firm

Through its efforts at SOX compliance, BlackRock, an investment firm with more than $450 billion in assets, discovered several deficiencies in its documents regarding job descriptions.

Job descriptions are an important component of SOX compliance because by clearly assigning tasks and responsibilities to appropriate positions, they contribute to efficient management of internal controls.

By using its SOX compliancy process as an opportunity to redo many important documents, including those pertaining to job descriptions, BlackRock has experienced benefits of quicker adjustment periods for new recruits, more tailored training programs, and more comprehensive employee evaluations.

This is just one example of how SOX has motivated and fostered system changes whose benefits extend beyond compliancy.[a]

[a] Stephen Wagner and Lee Dittmar, ''The Unexpected Benefits of Sarbanes-Oxley,'' *Harvard Business Review* (April 2006).

Although their fears turned out to be relatively unfounded, XBRL will allow organizations to compile data and create reports in a highly efficient manner, enabling compliance with tight time constraints.

Enterprise Resource Planning Software

The establishment and monitoring of internal controls is greatly facilitated when a company's processes are centralized rather than fragmented. ERP serves as a platform to integrate all of a company's departments and functions into one dynamic system. These systems are based primarily on accounting and financial data, making them relevant considerations in SOX compliancy planning.

Benefits of ERP. By integrating all information within one system, ERP eliminates the need to pass information and rekey data into new systems. This strategy has gained popularity because of its benefits for efficiency, data accuracy, and information management.

Companies that use ERP software are also able to benefit from improved communication and a heightened level of reporting efficiency. One centralized system ensures that access controls and activities can be monitored effectively and that all parties who require reports on such activities will be contacted.

TIPS AND TECHNIQUES

Criteria Checklist for ERP Selection for SOX-Compliant Companies

All publicly traded companies should consider these questions when selecting an ERP that will function compatibly with their SOX compliancy efforts:

TIPS AND TECHNIQUES (CONTINUED)

- ☐ Which Relational Database Management System (RDBMS) does the ERP work with?
- ☐ Are there built-in programs designed to handle integration?
- ☐ How is data warehousing addressed?
- ☐ Does the software support distributed data processing and parallel processing options?
- ☐ Is there an audit trail on key transactions?
- ☐ How many security layers are incorporated?
- ☐ What networking protocols does the software support?

TIPS AND TECHNIQUES

Strategies for Successful IT Compliance

Because IT plays such a vital role in SOX compliance, it is a good idea to understand the basic framework of how successful IT compliance comes about. Here is a systematic solution list for establishing successful IT control design when working toward SOX compliance:

- ☐ Evaluate current IT risk and control processes before rushing to replace them. It may be possible to maintain the current systems using supplements as necessary.
- ☐ Carefully assess in-house IT resources and seek expert advice where knowledge is lacking. A lack of experience could lead to wasted resources and even failed compliance.
- ☐ Focus only on those controls relevant to certification requirements.

Tips and Techniques (continued)

- ☐ Take this opportunity to identify, select, and implement an improved IT control framework.
- ☐ Look ahead to ensure sustainability. SOX compliance is an ongoing process. By planning for the future, a company can greatly minimize the continuing costs.
- ☐ Treat this as an investment in future assurances of accountability.

Benefits of IT in SOX Compliance

Few systems or processes within a company could not benefit from a reevaluation and revamping. Particularly in the IT department, many companies have been focused on downsizing in recent years, which has led to inefficient updates and monitoring.

As a result of previous neglect, some companies have found that SOX has demanded a great deal of resources. In efforts to meet the overall requirements presented by the Act, many companies have undergone extensive reforms to their IT systems, a process that is both costly and time consuming.

These changes can be viewed as business investments, however, because often they carry significant financial and service benefits. These additional advantages of IT SOX compliance include:

- *Advanced risk control that limits costly errors and deceits.* As with all SOX compliance efforts, eliminating the risk of ending up bankrupt like Enron, or financially crippled as Tyco International, is a valuable benefit. By establishing stronger controls and greater security, companies are able to prevent such dire fates and protect themselves, their investors, and their employees.

- *Improvement in IT systems due to increased demand.* The entire market is benefiting from the fact that increased demand and new requirements are fueling quick and exciting developments in information technology. Not only will these developments improve SOX compliance efforts, they are also serving to improve all areas of IT.
- *Improved organization of IT systems and applications.* Many companies have built their IT environments piece by piece as new requirements arose and new solutions developed. By compelling companies to organize and evaluate their IT systems and applications, SOX is providing them with a reason to improve their efficiency and eliminate unnecessary applications.
- *Increased IT understanding of executives.* Too often company executives are ignorant to the occurrences within their IT departments. By mandating that CEOs and CFOs certify the internal controls of their companies, SOX forces executives to learn more about IT. Increasing the knowledge base of the executives is important, especially in an area as vital as IT. Doing so will serve to improve the executives' ideas and understanding of the company, thereby improving the company and its ability to function.
- *Heightened level of communication among company members.* Too often large companies are siloed into smaller divisions that rarely interact and appear to function almost autonomously.

By forcing IT divisions to interact with other areas of the company, SOX compliancy establishes and improves channels of communication that can be employed later for other joint efforts.

- *Prevention of information loss and reduction of system violation risks.* One of the primary objectives of establishing IT controls is to protect the integrity of financial data and other SOX-related documents. Doing so will provide further benefits for compliant companies by creating organized systems of document retention and destruction, thereby increasing efficiency of all document-related activities.

Conclusion

Understanding IT and its role in SOX compliance is a big part of understanding SOX as a whole. Here is a review of some of the core concepts that were discussed in this chapter.

SOX compliance is integrally related to the development of a sound IT system, although the Act itself makes no direct mention of software. Companies will want to review their IT divisions to ensure that the technology being used maximizes their ability to test and monitor their controls efficiently.

During their compliance efforts, companies will use their IT divisions to help accelerated reporting requirement, certification requirements, internal control monitoring, and record keeping.

The IT division will follow a series of specific steps toward implementing the controls necessary for SOX compliance. These steps include planning through risk assessment, control design, monitoring, and communication.

Although SOX does not provide specific guidance in terms of how companies need to go about achieving compliance, there is information available through other best practices including COBIT, ITIL, NIST and ISO.

In order to manage compliance efforts and account for the lack of IT knowledge of some CEOs and CFOs, a system of subcertification has evolved. Although not officially recognized or required by the PCAOB or the SEC, subcertification allows the CIO to sign off on IT controls, thereby assuring the CEO and CFO of their efficacy.

SOX, even more than Y2K, has created an entire industry of software and technology inspired solely by the needs of those companies striving to achieve compliance. Choosing the right software the first time can help companies create efficient systems and tests as well as maintain a lower overall cost of compliance.

Finally, looking on the bright side, some benefits of SOX compliance extend outside of the scope of regulation. As companies reevaluate and develop new controls and processes, they are able to create more efficient systems, upgrade out-of-date software, and improve their document-protection processes.

Summary

- IT is integral to SOX compliance.
- Accelerated reporting, certification, and internal controls all require IT assistance.
- IT is directly related to the establishment of internal controls as required in Section 302 and Section 404.

Summary

- SOX requires the implementation of IT-developed controls.
- ISO/IEC, ITIL, and NIST are security best practices that can be instrumental in the establishment of controls.
- SOX compliance benefits companies by motivating them to reevaluate out-of-date or ineffective IT processes and systems.

CHAPTER 8

Beyond The American Corporation

After reading this chapter, you will be able to:

- Understand the challenge that the Sarbanes-Oxley Act (SOX) creates for outsourcing.
- Understand the unique challenges and advantages that small public companies face in SOX compliance.
- Understand voluntary compliance and its relevance for nonprofit organizations.

Introduction

Although its primary "target" may have been those corporations most likely to defraud investors, the impact of the Sarbanes-Oxley Act (SOX) actually extends much further. This chapter explores some of the widespread consequences that SOX is having outside the realm of large corporations.

Outsourcing Challenge

One of many conundrums presented by SOX was that in order to simplify and streamline business processes, it indirectly required companies to outsource more work while at the same time directly limiting their ability to do so safely.

SOX makes chief executive officers (CEOs) and chief financial officers (CFOs) directly responsible for any misrepresentations within the company's financial records, irrespective of who performed the actual activities. This means that regardless of whether a process was developed in house or by an outsourcer halfway across the world, the CEO/CFO is responsible if it does not meet the company's SOX requirements.

As a result, companies have had to reframe the way they think of outsourcing. Prior to SOX, a company would assign an activity to an outsourcing company and expect either the requested results or that the outsourcing company would assume responsibility. Now companies must think of outsourcers as extensions of their company. This changes the way that business is conducted.

IN THE REAL WORLD

Outsourcing Advantage of the Big Four

Perhaps the biggest benefit of SOX has been felt by the Big Four accounting firms. A survey released by the Association of Audit

In The Real World (continued)

Committee Members (AACM) indicates that the auditing fees of the Big Four more than doubled within the two years following 2002.

As more firms enter the market, the monopoly held by the Big Four will begin to decline. However, smaller firms face difficulties providing the same services because they do not have the same international reach or specific industry knowledge.

Some of the dissent against SOX is due to the fact that those same firms involved in scandals of the 1990s are now reaping the benefits.

When an Outsourcer Becomes SOX Relevant

To help companies and outsourcers navigate SOX compliance, the Public Companies Accounting Oversight Board (PCAOB) released the PCAOB attestation standard.[1] This standard provides an outline of the circumstances in which an outsourcer becomes part of the company's internal controls. There are four circumstances in which outsourcers may affect company controls.

1. *When the outsourcer affects how the company initiates any of its transactions.* As an event that directly impacts every financial step thereafter, transaction initiation has the potential to create a significant impact on the company's financial statements and is therefore in need of a control.
2. *When the outsourcer impacts how the company's transactions are processed or reported in the accounting records and other*

documents. By directly impacting the reporting procedure, this process is highly relevant to ensuring the accuracy of financial reports and other relevant documents.

3. *When the outsourcer affects how the company processes its transactions.* As with the initiation of a transaction, the outsourcer that creates impact on transaction processing also creates impact on financial documents and therefore must be included in the compliance efforts.
4. *When the outsourcer influences the creation of financial statements through the financial reporting process.* As in Step 2, this activity has the potential to create circumstances whereby the outsourcer could materially influence the integrity of the financial report.

Companies need to include their outsourcers as part of their internal control development and monitoring systems in these four circumstances. As outsourcers generally work with several companies, remaining accessible for several individual audits is not a viable option; it would require too much time and too many resources. As a solution, many outsourcing companies choose alternative routes to help in the compliance efforts of those who hire them.

Ways Outsourcers Can Aid in Compliance

Support companies can make it easier for publicly traded companies to hire them by taking steps toward their own SOX compliance. Specifically, companies that accept outsourcing contracts can hire external auditors to assess systems that are relevant to SOX-compliant companies and report on the efficiency of those systems in controlling risks.

Outsourcers can also have auditors test the efficacy of controls that they apply to those processes relevant to transactions of SOX-compliant companies.

By ensuring the efficacy of their own controls and providing their clients with a reliable report from a reputable external auditor, outsourcers better equip publicly traded companies to meet the demands of SOX compliance.

TIPS AND TECHNIQUES

Successful Outsourcing in Compliance with SOX

As mentioned, complications of the post-SOX corporate world can hinder outsourcing. The most important thing for companies that employ external services to remember is that outsourcing in no way diminishes or eliminates the responsibilities held by their CEOs and CFOs.

In order to outsource while still maintaining SOX compliance, executives must:

- *Fully understand their own responsibilities and duties.* These responsibilities do not change, regardless of whether the services are provided in house or through an external provider. CEOs/CFOs must ensure that they understand their responsibilities so that they can ensure the outsourcer enables them to meet those responsibilities.
- *Identify service provider activities that are significant.* As a further step toward ensuring that they are able to meet their own requirements successfully, CEOs/CFOs must understand which activities provided by the outsourcer are relevant to SOX compliance.

Tips and Techniques (continued)

- *Fully understand the procedures used by service providers in performance of those relevant activities.* When outsourcers provide services related to SOX compliance, CEOs/CFOs need to understand the providers' procedures and evaluate them to ensure that they are adequate.
- *Test and assess the results of all relevant services provided by the service provider.* Since CEOs/CFOs ultimately are responsible for the certification of the accuracy of financial statements, any services provided by outsourcers should be tested and assessed the same manner as if they were performed in house.

SAS 70

Statement on Auditing Standards No. 70 (SAS 70) was developed by the American Institute of Certified Public Accountants (AICPA) to help companies reconcile the difficulties of outsourcing within SOX compliance.

The relevant internal controls of those organizations that provide services to SOX-compliant companies must also be SOX compliant. When publicly traded companies outsource tasks related to their financial statements, their executive officers are still responsible for the accurate completion of those tasks. This means that with each audit of a company's internal controls; those tasks provided out of house must also be equally considered. In order to eliminate the need for individual audits each time a client is audited, a service provider can provide a SAS 70.

An SAS 70 certifies that the service organization has received an in-depth audit of its relevant internal controls. This allows the executives of those companies that use the services of the outsourcer to certify that their own financial statements are accurate. It also enables external auditors to attest to the outsourcer's internal control standards without having to visit it.

In addition to limiting the number of external audit requests that the service organization has to submit to, an SAS 70 also provides organizations with additional benefits. Obtaining such certification demonstrates initiative and provides quality assurance, which sets compliant organizations apart from their competitors. SAS 70 audits also provide organizations with useful insight into opportunities to improve their systems and processes, which can lead to greater efficiency and security.

IN THE REAL WORLD

SAS 70 Report Contents

In the post-SOX world, outsourcing is not as easy as it once was. Now companies must consider whether those tasks that they are outsourcing are relevant to their compliance efforts and, if they are, how they will monitor the controls established to protect them.

Even though the tasks are completed out of house, SOX does not release CEOs/CFOs from their role and responsibility over the creation and certification of controls. This means that those who employ outsourcing services must have a method of monitoring and testing the controls of the outsource company.

One method would be to include the outsource company in the audit process conducted by the company. Although this would serve to

IN THE REAL WORLD (CONTINUED)

evaluate the controls, conducting off-site audits is costly and time consuming.

Such situations are not ideal for the outsource company either, as it would have to submit to audits for each of its many clients. Instead, the best option is for the outsourced-to company to obtain an SAS 70.

An SAS 70 provides publicly traded companies with assurance that sufficient internal controls are being managed within their out-of-house service providers. As a cost- and time-effective alternative to individual audits, an SAS 70 audit report is presented to SOX-compliant companies to be included in their evaluations.

There are two types of SAS 70 reports:

1. *Type I.* Within a Type I SAS 70 report is information regarding a service organization's controls at a specific point in time. This report includes the service organization's description of its systems and controls, the service organization's outline of its internal controls, and the auditor's opinion of the internal controls and their efficacy.
2. *Type II.* In addition to a description of the controls, a Type II SAS 70 report also includes the details of control testing that had been completed over a lengthy period of time (at least six months). This report includes not only a description of the systems and the auditor's opinion on their efficacy, but also a description of the auditor's control tests and a compilation of the results.

Although outsourcing is made a little more challenging in the post-SOX world, very few companies complete all tasks solely in house. For this reason, at least a portion of most CEO/CFO control certifications rely on those controls established by external bodies outside of their domain. Companies can reconcile their need to outsource with the requirement to certify the efficacy of controls by obtaining an SAS report from the external service provider.

Uniqueness of Small Businesses

Another area of dissent for those who disagree with SOX and its provisions is the fact that small companies feel its financial burden disproportionately. These dissenters argue that the manner in which SOX compliance is framed does not adequately account for resources available to small companies.

The establishment and maintenance of a compliance system requires many set costs that do not relate to the size of the company, such as the purchasing of software and outsourcing fees. Thus, the cost of compliance does not decrease incrementally depending on company size. Therefore, small businesses are forced to spend a greater proportion of their annual revenue on compliance costs.

It is further argued that SOX creates a boundary between small companies and their ability to go public because of the difficulty they have in achieving compliance. Some fear that this will stifle future business development and potentially strangle the market. The argument is that by preventing small companies from going public, SOX will prevent their acquisition of further funds and therefore hamper their ability to grow.

Those who take this argument to its fullest believe that should SOX prevent all small businesses from listing, it could prevent any large companies from developing, thereby hurting the market. This would be completely contrary to the spirit of the Act, which seeks to protect the health of the market.

It is true that small businesses have a difficult time under SOX; an Office of Government Commerce (OGC) study found that companies with under $700 million in annual revenues suffer a disproportionate financial burden in achieving SOX compliance.[2]

It is also true that some companies have delisted, claiming SOX requirements and the associated costs as a major factor. However, these companies are mostly very small, with under $30 million in market capitalization. Fewer than 20% of companies that have declined to go public cite SOX as a reason that they remain private.

Those small businesses that have either chosen to remain listed or to initiate their initial public offering (IPO) are receiving special consideration. The Securities and Exchange Commission (SEC) and the PCAOB have not been insensitive to the increased burden faced by small and midsize businesses. For this reason, compliance dates for companies with less than $75 million have been extended repeatedly.

Of course, it is unlikely that SOX compliance will stand in the way of any small companies ever listing on the market. Although small companies face unique challenges in meeting the regulations, their difficulties have not fallen upon deaf ears. For example, the PCAOB has extended compliance dates for companies under $75 million to provide extra time for resource generation and planning. This extension also has the unintended benefit of allowing small businesses to ride on the coattails of those that went before them. They are able to learn from the costly mistakes made by larger companies in their first year of compliance, thereby saving both time and money. Additionally, outsourcers and products in both the information technology (IT) and other SOX-compliance–supporting industries may be less expensive for small businesses that are coming in the wake of the compliance rush.

Like all other companies impacted by SOX, these service providers have needed time to organize themselves and improve their efficiencies. These changes will result in greater value for the company. Small businesses will also benefit from a lessening of SOX service provider competition, now that the largest companies are in the maintenance stage of their compliance efforts.

Unique Challenges and Advantages of Small Companies

While most of the discussion around small businesses has centered around the challenges and hurdles that they face in complying with SOX, they also bring to the table some advantages when it comes to compliance. This section explores these advantages as well as challenges that are unique to small businesses vis-à-vis SOX.

Advantages

- *Small companies can create a greater degree of control than large ones.* Given their size in terms of divisions, subsidaries, and staff, small companies may have an easier time controlling their SOX compliance efforts than larger companies do.
- *Small companies can facilitate a greater deal of transparency to executives.* Again, because of their size, smaller companies may have an easier time maintaining the involvement of the executives in the execution of SOX-related controls. As a result, fewer controls will have to be established to guarantee to the CEO/CFO that financial documents that are certified are certifying accurate information.

Challenges

- *Greater financial burden because obtaining sufficient funds can be difficult.* Given their limited ability to raise capital, some small companies may have a difficult time locating the financial resources required to achieve first-time and ongoing compliance.
- *Fewer staffing resources on hand; therefore, more outsourcing required.* Similar to the effects of severe downsourcing in large companies, many small companies simply do not have the number of people required to achieve SOX compliance through in-house efforts. As a result, a greater deal of outsourcing is often required, which can create additional financial stress.
- *Difficulty segregating duties and creating a separate audit committee because of the limited people involved in the company.* Continuing compliance with SOX requires that a company establish an independent audit committee and that activities related to financial information maintain sufficient segregation of duty. In small companies there are often too few employees to meet either of these requirements adequately.
- *Increased danger of management intervention to create the appearance that objectives have been met.* Because management is more directly involved in the business processes, it is possible that management will be tempted to override processes in order to mimic objective compliance. Not only does this put the company at risk, it is also counter to the spirit of SOX.

Financial Bottom Line

A survey conducted by SAP listed the financial effects that some small businesses have faced in their efforts toward compliance.[3] According to the findings, 18% of companies that responded had been forced to cut costs in marketing and research and/or development to divert funds to their SOX compliancy efforts.

Receiving an Extension

The same survey conducted discovered the ways in which small companies were taking advantage of their extra year. The results included:

- 54% reevaluated their plans and invested more resources into planning.
- 53% hired external consultants to create compliance plans.
- 10% intend to ignore SOX regulations and hope that small businesses will eventually be made exempt altogether.

Formal and Informal Controls

When establishing a strategy for SOX compliance, companies have the option of establishing formal or informal controls to secure their processes. By establishing formal controls, a company is able to instill structure and responsibility in their SOX compliance efforts. With proper implementation, formal controls provide all employees with a clear idea of their expectations and roles. Formal controls also ensure that the overall SOX compliance effort is complete and that it does not contain any holes.

While informal controls can create difficulty because they are difficult to enforce consistently, they do have value in that they provide flexibility and, in some cases, cost efficiency. The degree to which informal controls can be applied will depend on the company's organizational model. Those companies that are small enough for direct management interaction with all company activities will be more able to incorporate informal controls than larger companies.

Regardless of size, companies do have to establish a minimum set of formal controls for those SOX compliance efforts that require control documentation and formal evaluation of control efficacy.

IN THE REAL WORLD

Foley & Lardner Survey

Few would argue that SOX compliance is a costly venture. According to a survey of 32 midsize companies conducted by the law firm Foley & Lardner, public companies with annual revenues under $1 billion had their annual costs increase by 130%.[a] These increases are being directly attributed to legislative fallouts from corporate scandals including SOX and the new SEC rules. Many feel that these increased costs will be passed on to customers and shareholders.

The survey also found that a related implication is that fewer companies see going public as providing enough benefit to outweigh compliance problems. Although there has been no significant diminution in the number of companies that issues initial public offerings each year, it is feared that the number will slowly decrease as alternative markets become more viable.

[a] "The Increased Financial and Non-Financial Cost of Staying Public," 2003 (www.foleylardner.com).

Recommendations for Small Businesses from COSO

In 2006, the Committee of Sponsoring Organizations (COSO) published *Internal Control over Financial Reporting—Guidance for Smaller Public Companies*.[4] This document was designed to address the assertions that COSO's internal control framework had not been sufficiently tailored for small businesses. Although this document does not alter the COSO framework at all, it does provide guidance for small companies looking to apply it to their compliance efforts.

The most important guidance that COSO offers is to give small companies "permission" to adjust their compliance efforts to suit their unique needs rather than trying to change their businesses to suit compliance. In particular, small companies can limit the documentation that they generate, take a more holistic approach to their compliance efforts, and address their limited segregation of duty with additional controls rather than additional company members.

Effectively scaling documentation. Small companies have the advantage of fewer employees and greater management interaction. With a less complicated business structures, the board of directors is better able to perform oversight responsibilities without the assistance of a high volume of documentation. Closer working relationships and fewer levels of management also allow smaller companies to avoid excessive documentation regarding the controls behind their financial reporting.

Although documentation of internal controls is always necessary to some extent, the volume can reflect the complexity and size of the company. It is important that small companies understand that SOX compliance requires only that sufficient documentation exist to support the CEO/CFO and auditor evaluation of the controls, rather than assuming that they require the same amount of documentation as large companies.

Viewing internal controls as a holistic system. By understanding that the internal controls work together to ensure the accuracy of the financial reports, small companies can better integrate their compliance efforts. Establishing a system in which each control is meant to function at the highest level of accuracy on its own will involve overdevelopment and unnecessary costs.

Instead, small companies should recognize that while circumstantial deficiency may exist in one control, the control is still considered effective as long as another control will prevent the financial statements from being adversely effected.

By recognizing that each control does not have to work perfectly every time, but rather that the system must function effectively as a whole, small companies will be better able to build a more cost-effective plan for compliance.

Addressing limited segregation of duties. One of the most important points of guidance is how to help small businesses achieve compliance and implement effective controls in spite of being unable to create a great deal of duty segregation. Because smaller companies have a limited staff pool in which to assign duties, they can have difficulty creating a sufficient segregation of tasks. These companies will be required to implement controls designed directly to compensate for this fact.

- Management should review reports of detail transactions that have been initiated by staff when such duties have not been sufficiently segregated. This review will serve to provide early identification and correction of improper transactions.
- Management should compare asset counts and accounting records when there is limited segregation of duties involving inventory and other assets. Doing so will allow the company to verify that the assets and accounts contain matching data, as well as take actions in those situations where inconsistencies arise.

Additionally, through this document COSO outlines 26 guidelines that will help small businesses implement the five-part framework.

Control environment. By creating a culture of compliance, small businesses will be more efficient in applying their compliance efforts. Ensuring that ethics and integrity are valued within the company is very important, especially within management. It is also important that companies align their objectives, management styles, organizational structure, and hiring decisions with their compliance efforts. This means, for example, that all company members understand the importance of compliance and are provided with appropriate education and tasks to help the company achieve its goal.

- *Risk assessment.* In order to assess risks effectively, a small company must clearly establish its objectives and then narrow its focus toward identifying risks that could lead to misstatements of financial reports by either fraud or error.
- *Control activities.* Small businesses can adjust their efforts at developing control activities by focusing only on those that are

identified as providing material risks. Control development should be balanced with budgeting factors and consideration should be given to purchasing template software that will increase efficiency.

- *Communication.* As a direct benefit of the limited employee base, small companies are better able to communicate internally effectively without the need for establishing expensive systems. By establishing a clear framework and time frame to support identifying, capturing, and distributing information to relevant parties, small companies can ensure that internal control information and objectives are received by those who require the information.
- *Monitoring.* COSO recommends that small businesses adopt a system in which they continually monitor and evaluate their highest-risk controls. This is achievable because of their smaller size, which also helps ensure that those parties involved in correcting deficient controls will understand and remedy the problem in a timely manner.

TIPS AND TECHNIQUES

IPOs and SOX Compliance

SOX impacts all companies that are listed on the U.S. markets, including those releasing their IPO. Companies that are listing on a public market for the first time are required to fulfill compliance with SOX once they have filed their registration statement with the SEC.

TIPS AND TECHNIQUES (CONTINUED)

It is not a requirement of the Act that the company have any investors, only that the company is listed on the market. This means that those companies that are planning an IPO should initiate their SOX strategy well in advance. One year is generally considered a sufficient amount of time.

Small businesses have been singled out as having particular difficulty obtaining SOX compliance due to not only their limited revenue but also the limited size of their organizational structure. The struggles faced by these companies have not been ignored. In order to help combat the high cost of compliance, companies with annual revenues under $75 million were granted an extension on their compliance deadlines.

These companies have also received specific guidelines from COSO to help them tailor their compliance efforts to match their size and to assist them in compliance difficulties related to company organization.

Impact on Foreign Issuers

Foreign issuers are required to comply with SOX if they also file SEC annual reports 20-F or 40-F. Although the initial compliance date for foreign issuers was set for July 15, 2006, the SEC announced on March 2, 2005, that it would extend the compliance date for foreign issuers to 90 days after the first fiscal year ending on or before July 15, 2006.

Non-U.S. Framework: Turnbull

Although no mandates exist that require foreign issuers to use a U.S. framework, many choose to do so. It is reasonable to expect, and has been the general experience, that non-U.S. frameworks can create unnecessary complexities.

Unlike SOX compliance, the United Kingdom's Combined Code on Corporate Governance asks companies either to comply with regulations or to offer sufficient explanation otherwise. Cooperation with this regulation is facilitated by the Turnbull framework.

In general, the Combined Code of Corporate Governance provides companies with greater flexibility than that which is found under SOX. As a result, companies that have implemented Turnbull or other non-U.S. frameworks may not have sufficient framework designs to achieve SOX compliance.

Turnbull provides guidance for not only all internal control over financial reporting, but also all internal controls within a company. This system encourages a risk-based approach and emphasizes holistic internal control developments. Although not designed as a SOX framework, Turnbull can be effective if the company is willing to exert additional effort in those areas not covered in Turnbull but required by SOX.

By allowing foreign issuers over one year preparation time, the SEC was attempting to ease the additional burdens they faced. The benefits of a later compliance date included:

- Avoidance of the rush faced by large companies and, therefore, reprieve from the high competition for service providers

- Increased access to software technology developed during the first year
- Improved systems and increased volume of compliance information over those required to comply in first year
- More time to reconcile SOX regulations with conflicts in home-country regulations, laws, and customs

However, no amount of extra time would be enough to eliminate all of the concerns foreign issuers faced with compliance. For example, one of the biggest concerns for foreign issuers is the increased personal responsibility assumed by CEOs and CFOs under SOX. This responsibility does not fit with many foreign business styles, and no amount of compliance extensions will reconcile the differences.

Conflicts between SOX Compliance and Foreign Issuers

Exporting U.S. legislation and anticipating easy compliance is not a realistic expectation. Other countries not only have their own rules and regulations governing businesses, they also have varying customs and business styles that may not integrate well with SOX compliance.

Unlike the United States where shareholder interests and profits are held in high regard, other countries, such as Japan, place their focus on company-related goals, such as expanding power and market share. This difference of paradigm has created conflict with foreign issuers seeking compliance because SOX requires them to switch business objectives and place more weight on the needs of the shareholder.

IN THE REAL WORLD

J-SOX and the Japanese Market

In November 2006, the Financial Services Agency of Japan (a rough counterpart to the SEC) released a governance framework as an answer to SOX. Although written with similar intentions in mind, J-SOX, as it has come to be known, reflects the unique landscape of the Japanese economy. One of the biggest distinctions is that in Japan, large industrial groups are more popular than stand-alone companies are. The new regulations are expected to encourage these groups to consolidate subsidiaries into larger units.

Additionally, governments of many countries have resented the requirement that their public accounting firms register with the U.S. PCAOB. Such a requirement is viewed as an usurpation of their own responsibilities.

IN THE REAL WORLD

Legal and Civil Vulnerability

A major concern that foreign companies face when listing through American Depository Receipts (ADRs) is the risk of U.S. judges applying U.S. law extraterritorially when claims are brought by non-U.S. plaintiffs. In cases of this nature, U.S. judges have been willing to hear claims even when the activity was committed outside of the United States by a non-U.S. citizen against a non-U.S. citizen. The only requirement seems to be that the effects of the conduct are sufficiently severe in the United States.

American Depository Receipts

An ADR is a stock that trades on the U.S. markets but represents a specified number of shares in a foreign corporation. These receipts allow foreign issuers to raise capital by having their shares bought and sold on U.S. markets. ADRs also enable investor to purchase foreign shares with ease.

In general, ADRs are listed on the U.S. markets when U.S. banks purchase a bulk lot of shares from the company and reissue them onto the New York Stock Exchange (NYSE), American Stock Exchange (AMEX), or National Association of Securities Dealers Automated Quotations System (NASDAQ). These banks protect their initial investment by requiring that the company provide detailed financial information that is both up to date and accurate.

Delving a little deeper into the issue, three levels of ADRs exist. Level 1 ADRs have loose requirements from the SEC and are traded via a dealer network rather than a formal exchange such as NYSE, Toronto Stock Exchange (TSX), and AMEX.

Level 2 ADRs are listed on the NASDQ and have slightly more strict SEC regulations than Level 1, but Level 3 ADRs are the most regulated. These ADRs reach the U.S. markets when an issuer floats a public offering on the U.S. exchanges. Foreign companies engage in Level 3 ADRs, despite their heavy SEC requirements, because of their potential to raise capital and gain visibility.

IN THE REAL WORLD

Global Depositary Receipts

As an alternative to ADRs, Global Depositary Receipts (GDRs) have experienced a 15% increase since the inception of SOX. This increase may be at least partially related to the increased requirements placed on those non-U.S. companies that enter the U.S. markets.

Achieving Compliance

Foreign issuers are likely to have the most difficult time of all companies compelled to comply with SOX. As written, the Act does not take into consideration different countries and their social and economic values. As a result, many companies have trouble reconciling SOX requirements with the sometimes competing requirements of their own country's regulations.

To see how SOX compares with corporate governance regulations in other countries, visit www.sec.gov/news/speech/2006/spch091106et.htm.

IN THE REAL WORLD

Independent Audit Committees and Civil Law Regimes

Foreign issuers that exist under a civil law regime object to complying with SOX requirements that necessitate the formation

In The Real World (continued)

of an independent audit committee. The reason for their objection is that doing so would give labor representatives serving on the audit committee responsibilities and access to information that would increase labor's bargaining power. Further objection to the establishment of an independent audit committee is that it creates a conflict with their own country's requirement for codetermination.

Although several foreign issuing companies are working well with the requirements mandated by SOX, there is an overwhelming sense that the general opinion is one of displeasure.

A great fear is that foreign companies will pull out of the U.S. markets, which would result in less market diversity, displeasing investors and possibly weakening the markets themselves. However, there is no clear indication (statistically speaking) that companies are delisting at a greater rate post-SOX than they were before. In addition, it is important to note that even though a company may delist from the U.S. markets, they are not necessarily exempt from SOX-compliance regulations. As long as 300 U.S. investors, or more, own shares of their stocks, the company is still compelled to comply with the Act.

Impact on Nonprofit Organizations

Although not publicly traded or reliant on the confidence of investors, not-for-profit organizations are making a strong move toward voluntary SOX compliance. This is partially the result of the fact that SOX reminded nonprofits that their existence is based on the trust of the public and their constituents.

Voluntary Compliance

As an ideal, SOX compliance is expected to be viewed as the new standard in corporate governance. To this end, companies that are not legally compelled to comply with SOX standards can still benefit from its recommendations. It is because of these benefits that several non–publicly traded companies and organizations have adopted frameworks that mirror SOX compliance.

In addition, in some circumstances, organizations other than the PCAOB demand SOX compliance as part of their contract of agreements with a non–publicly traded company. For example, these circumstances include situations where a private company seeks funds through venture capital funding or commercial loans. It is important to remember, however, that under these circumstances, SOX compliance or noncompliance is not a legal consideration.

Benefits of Voluntary Compliance

Throughout this book we have discussed many of the benefits that SOX-compliant companies can look forward to. Those companies that choose voluntarily to comply with SOX will feel not only those benefits, but also benefits associated with their voluntary status.

One the greatest benefits of voluntary compliance is the fact that there is no risk; executives do not risk jail time under SOX even if the statements they sign are fraudulent.

Voluntary compliance also provides the organization with a great boost in public image. Because organizations that comply voluntarily present an image of taking initiative and proactive behavior, they look good. This effectively ensures that not-for-profit organizations are able to bask in the ethical image provided by compliance without enduring any of the risks.

Additional benefits include:

- *Development of new controls.* Nonprofit organizations have as much need as for-profit companies do for internal controls to ensure the integrity of their financial reports. By working toward voluntary SOX compliance, these companies are able to take advantage of SOX-related frameworks such as Control Objectives for Information and Related Technology (COBIT) and COSO, thereby gaining greater control over their operations and fostering the confidence of those who invest their time and money in their causes.
- *Reevaluation of current controls.* By voluntarily complying with SOX standards, nonprofit organizations are able to streamline their current controls and the systems in place to monitor them. This can lead to increased efficiency and greater productivity through the redesign of outdated controls.
- *Greater financial organization.* SOX compliance encourages companies to gain greater control over their financial documents and their organization. By creating systems to regulate the retention, destruction, and communication of financial information, nonprofit organizations can streamline every finance-related process, from taxes to reporting.

- *Protecting against fraud.* All organizations are at risk of fraud and other criminal activities. Unfortunately, when such activities occur within nonprofit organizations, they evoke increased levels of community disdain and outrage. By increasing security and antifraud protections, SOX compliance efforts enable nonprofit organizations to maintain their ethical image and protect themselves against the dangers of fraud.

TIPS AND TECHNIQUES

Steps for Nonprofits Looking into Voluntary Compliance

Step 1. *Eliminate insider transactions and conflicts of interest.*

- Comply with regulations regarding director and executive compensation and benefits.
- Prohibit directors and executives from receiving personal loans.

Step 2. *Establish an independent and competent audit committee.*

- Annually conduct an external financial audit.
- Ensure audit committee members are free of conflict of interest.
- Ensure that that least one board member is a financial expert and the rest receive financial literacy training.

Step 3. *Clearly outline the auditor responsibilities.*

- Limit auditor contracts to five years.
- Do not use the auditing firm for any nonauditing services.
- Include conflict-of-interest enforcement in the audit committee's roles.

Tips and Techniques (continued)

Step 4. *Comply with necessary disclosures.*

- Disclose Forms 990 and 990-PF, preferably using electronic filing.
- Disclose audited financial statements.

Step 5. *Ensure whistle-blower protection.*

- Design formal policies to deal with complaints and suspicions, ensuring that proper consideration is given to preventing retaliation.
- Educate all organization members and employees regarding the policies.
- Ensure that the policies are consistently enforced.

Step 6. *Prevent document destruction.*

- Design formal policies that clearly regulate document retention and destruction.
- Ensure that the policies include consideration for paper documentation, electronic files, and audio files including voice mail.

Future Regulations

Many companies that are currently working toward voluntary compliance believe that their efforts are simply preemptive for regulations that are soon to come. Future regulations for nonprofit sector organizations could include:

- Restrictions on compensation for governing board members
- Requirement of mandatory audits for organizations over $250,000 in annual revenue
- Requirement that CEOs comply with SOX 404 certification

IN THE REAL WORLD

University of Pittsburgh Medical Center

Until recently the University of Pittsburgh Medical Center (UPMC) had a strict policy of releasing only as much information as required by law. Now the UPMC claims the title of the first nonprofit health care organization to become voluntarily compliant with SOX.

The challenge for the UPMC was adapting SOX to suit a nonprofit organization when it had been designed for publicly traded companies. For the UPMC, not all requirements regarding disclosing stock transactions were applicable. In addition, because nonprofits are not under the jurisdiction of the SEC, the UPMC had to choose an alternate method of disclosing financial information. The solution for UPMC has been to post financial data on its Web site.

One of the greatest benefits that the UPMC has found is that SOX compliance has encouraged it to complete steps to integrate its revenue cycle systems, which are designed to increase efficiency. The hospital estimates that through such efforts, it saves $1.5 million each year.[a]

[a] "Adhering to Best Business Practices," University of Pittsburgh Medical Center, *Extra* (June 2006).

Conclusion

SOX is a very wide-reaching and powerful act. Few other pieces of legislation are able to impact as many groups that are outside of their prescribed scope or to create as significant and varied of an impact for those within their realm.

This chapter has discussed the important issues that surround SOX compliancy and outsourcing, small businesses, foreign issuers, and not-for-profit organizations. In terms of outsourcing, the most significant issue is that companies are not absolved of their SOX compliance requirements even if the process is performed by an outside provider. This creates the necessity of SAS 70s and other measures to ensure that outsourcers have established and are maintaining adequate security controls.

Small, publicly traded companies also face a challenge in achieving compliance, but for them the challenge is money. Small companies carry a disproportionate amount of compliance cost compared to their relative size. This can mean financial hardship and also the impossibility of compliance if the funds cannot be found. The challenges faced by small companies have not gone unnoticed; in addition to receiving a compliance extension, COSO has also issued specific steps that small companies can take to tailor their compliance efforts to their size.

In terms of foreign issuers, the compliance problem is one of conflicting regulations and anger over exceeded jurisdiction. SOX requires that all companies traded on U.S. markets, including foreign issuers that are sold under ADRs, comply with its regulations.

Finally, not-for-profit organizations, although not compelled to obtain compliance in any legal sense, are becoming more conscious of their own governance practices as awareness of compliance benefits has spread.

Summary

- SOX creates a significant impact on outsourcers because they too must be included in the evaluation of a company's controls. This has led to the widespread use of SAS 70s.

- Small companies that are publicly traded have been given special consideration and an extended compliance deadline to help them manage the high costs of compliance.
- All companies traded on American markets, including foreign issuers, are required to comply with the SOX Act. Many foreign companies have found difficulty in reconciling SOX requirements with competing requirements from their own nations.
- Not-for-profit organizations can better serve their donors by proving a commitment to good governance practices.

Notes

1. More information regarding PCAOB Attestation Standards can be found at www.pcaobus.org/Standards/Interim_Standards/Attestation_Standards/index.aspx.
2. Senators Olympia Snowe and Michael Enzi, August 2005.
3. www.sap.com.
4. COSO, "Internal Control over Financial Reporting—Guidance for Smaller Public Companies," 2006. Committee of Sponsoring Organizations of the Treadway Commission, www.coso.org.

Afterword

Fifteen years ago, as I was starting my career, many companies were making poor decisions that would eventually lead to their demise. We all know about the scandals that led to the Sarbanes-Oxley Act (SOX), but it takes more than knowing about them to prevent them; it takes understanding.

In my line of work I have realized that the more years that we get under our belts, the more that we understand SOX, its nuances, challenges, and benefits.

No one understands this Act better than my colleague Sanjay. He has worked with SOX as a consultant and as the developer of the SOX Institute. He has striven to educate and inform people and to make SOX compliance understandable.

The SOX Institute's mission has been to bridge the gap between consultant and company—to ensure that everyone involved in SOX compliance has the information that they need to contribute to its success.

Sanjay has made it his personal goal to educate people at every turn. Through speeches, articles, and books, he has worked to identify holes in knowledge bases and fill them with his expertise and well-chosen words.

I am so happy that he was inspired to write this book. Adding to the wealth of information that he has already shared with the public, this book serves the important role of focusing in on the people who need to understand SOX best—the ones whose lives are impacted by it every business day.

Perhaps you read this book because you are a CEO looking for guidance on how to keep your company on track. Or maybe you are a recent grad looking for the information that will enable you to look intelligent at your first job interview. Regardless of your situation, this book provided you with the insights you needed to understand SOX.

Now that you have read through it (unless you're like me and you're starting from the back), I'm sure that you'll agree that SOX now seems a lot more manageable and a lot less daunting than it did before.

That is what the goal of this book has been: to equip you with the information to feel comfortable with the concepts of SOX. The parts of this book that will have stood out are going to be different for every reader. I would like to share those parts that have stuck out as most relevant to me.

The key principles that you learned about in Chapter 1 are meant to inspire you through every step of compliance. They are the spirit of SOX: integrity, accountability, and accuracy. Keep these principles in the forefront of your mind and allow them to guide every discussion you have about SOX and every decision that you make. These are the principles that we need to strive toward in every endeavor, and this Act is meant to embody them.

I was also very drawn to the sections related to cost-effective compliance strategies. Making SOX cost effective is a struggle that companies, consultants, and even auditors face every day. We have to balance the efforts to achieve the greatest controls and the most accurate systems with the understanding that businesses must remain viable as well as ethical.

I am happy to see that the costs of compliance have become more controlled in recent years. I look forward to seeing even greater progress made in this area, and, after reading this book, I'm sure you are able to understand the importance and methods for these improvements.

Of course, I could not neglect my own area of special fondness, information technology (IT). What I respect most about Sanjay's style of writing is his ability to capture the essence of something without drowning it in too much detail. His IT section takes everything that I do and packages it neatly for delivery into your mind.

The IT-related chapters will be your best friends and companions as new products emerge to create greater efficiencies for SOX compliance. It is an exciting time, and you are now able to join in on the dialogue and understand the events as they unfold.

Now that you've read through the text for the first time, I would encourage you to keep this book close at hand. As SOX compliance grows and changes, and as your knowledge base expands, you will want to return to these pages frequently.

One of the greatest features that I find of Sanjay's books, and this one is no exception, is that the information is simple to locate when I need a quick reference. The table of contents, summaries, and index all help to point me to that tidbit of information that I want to read one more time.

And often I find that my book is so dog-eared that I purchase two copies—one to sit on my shelf and look impressive and a second for me to use and abuse as I carry it on my own journey with SOX.

Robert J. Schwind, CISA, CSOXP®
President and CEO, GKBN Technologies
Vice President, Programs, ISACA, Hudson Valley

APPENDIX

Summary of the Sarbanes-Oxley Act

Title I—Public Company Accounting Oversight Board

The sections within Title I establish the Public Company Accounting Oversight Board (PCAOB). This nonprofit organization was established to oversee the public auditors and their activities.

The sections of Title I designate the PCAOB's powers and jurisdictions, both domestic and foreign. In general, the PCAOB has been directed to register public accounting firms, establish auditing standards, inspect registered public accounting firms, and lead investigations as well as disciplinary proceedings.

The sections of Title I are:

Section 101. Establishment; administration provisions

Section 102. Registration with the board

Section 103. Auditing, quality control, and independence standards

Section 104. Inspections of registered public accounting firms

Section 105. Investigations and disciplinary proceedings

Section 106. Foreign public accounting firms

Section 107. Commission oversight of the board

Section 108. Accounting standards

Section 109. Funding

Title II—Auditor Independence

The sections within Title II regulate auditors. A principle focus of this title is that conflicts of interest are prevented to ensure that the auditors provide unbiased assessments.

A major component to preventing conflicts of interest is the establishment of clear guidelines prohibiting auditors from providing extra services to companies. These include bookkeeping, appraisal, actuarial, broker, and legal services, among many others.

In a further effort to distance the auditor from having a vested interest in the company, this title also requires audit partner rotation and bans auditors from joining a company for a minimum of one year after providing services.

The sections of Title II are:

Section 201. Services outside the scope of practice of auditors

Section 202. Preapproval requirements

Section 203. Audit partner rotation

Section 204. Auditor reports to audit committees

Section 205. Conforming amendments

Section 206. Conflicts of interest

Section 207. Study of mandatory rotation of registered public accounting firms

Section 208. Commission authority

Section 209. Considerations by appropriate State regulatory authorities

Title III—Corporate Responsibility

Title III establishes regulations to ensure that only accurate financial records are distributed to the public. To this end, the sections of Title III require that companies establish an independent special audit committee. This section also lays out the requirement that chief executive officers (CEOs) and chief financial officers (CFOs) certify the accuracy of the financial reports filed with the Securities and Exchange Commission (SEC), that they verify the efficacy of the company's internal controls, and that they report on any changes.

Title III also creates limits regarding bonuses and stock trades for executive members. If the company must issue a restatement of its financial records, then the executive members may be required to forfeit some bonuses that they received during the relevant period.

The sections of Title III are:

Section 301. Public company audit committees

Section 302. Corporate responsibility for financial reports

Section 303. Improper influence on conduct of audits

Section 304. Forfeiture of certain bonuses and profits

Section 305. Officer and director bars and penalties

Section 306. Insider trades during pension fund blackout periods

Section 307. Rules of professional responsibility for attorneys

Section 308. Fair funds for investors

Title IV—Enhanced Financial Disclosures

Title IV creates further regulations to enhance the transparency and accuracy of financial disclosures. It requires that all material financial transactions be reported to eliminate misrepresentations. This includes both adjustments and off–balance sheet transactions.

Title IV also requires that financial activities of the executives be made more transparent by banning personal loans to executives and requiring disclosure of insider share trades.

The sections of Title IV are:

Section 401. Disclosures in periodic reports

Section 402. Enhanced conflict of interest provisions

Section 403. Disclosures of transactions involving management and principal stockholders

Section 404. Management assessment of internal controls

Section 405. Exemption

Section 406. Code of ethics for senior financial officers

Section 407. Disclosure of audit committee financial expert

Section 408. Enhanced review of periodic disclosures by issuers

Section 409. Real time issuer disclosures

Title V—Analyst Conflicts of Interest

Title V contains only one section and is dedicated solely to the treatment of analysts and protecting their ability to pass negative reports. This section also works to eliminate conflicts of interest that could produce biased reports by limiting the involvement that investment bankers can have with analysts.

The Title V section is:

Section 501. Treatment of securities analysts by registered securities associations and national securities exchanges

Title VI—Commission Resources and Authority

Title IV deals with the SEC, its abilities, and its jurisdiction. It expands the powers of the SEC and gives it the ability to hire more manpower to oversee auditors and audit firms.

The sections of Title VI are:

Section 601. Authorization of appropriations

Section 602. Appearance and practice before the Commission

Section 603. Federal court authority to impose penny stock bars

Section 604. Qualifications of associated persons of brokers and dealers

Title VII—Studies and Reports

The sections of Title VII initiate the authorization of studies and reports designed to further facilitate the interests of SOX compliance. These reports assess public accounting firms, credit ranking agencies, and investment banks in their influence on the public markets and relevant issues, including fraud.

The sections of Title VII are:

Section 701. Government Accounting Office (GAO) study and report regarding consolidation of public accounting firms

Section 702. Commission study and report regarding credit rating agencies

Section 703. Study and report on violators and violations

Section 704. Study of enforcement actions

Section 705. Study of investment banks

Title VIII—Corporate and Criminal Fraud Accountability

Title VIII contains sections that impose criminal penalties and extends the statute of limitation for acts of fraud. It also provides protection for whistle-blowers. The penalties under Title VIII are for individuals who knowingly falsify or destroy financial records, as well as for auditors who fail to maintain their records for the five-year minimum.

In terms of whistle-blowers, this title requires that companies facilitate the reporting actions of whistle-blowers as well as protect them from retaliation. Title VIII also states the specific retributions that whistle-blowers can expect if they experience wrongful treatment as a result of their actions.

The sections of Title VIII are:

Section 801. Short title

Section 802. Criminal penalties for altering documents

Section 803. Debts nondischargeable if incurred in violation of securities fraud laws

Section 804. Statute of limitations for securities fraud

Section 805. Review of Federal Sentencing Guidelines for obstruction of justice and extensive criminal fraud

Section 806. Protection for employees of publicly traded companies who provide evidence of fraud

Section 807. Criminal penalties for defrauding shareholders of publicly traded companies

Title IX—White-Collar Crime Penalty Enhancements

Title IX increases criminal penalties for white-collar crimes, such as mail and wire fraud. This title also contains the legal penalties for executives who do not certify the accuracy of the company's financial reports or who certify reports that do meet SOX compliance standards.

The sections of Title IX are:

Section 901. Short title

Section 902. Attempts and conspiracies to commit criminal fraud offenses

Section 903. Criminal penalties for mail and wire fraud.

Section 904. Criminal penalties for violations of the Employee Retirement Income Security Act of 1974

Section 905. Amendment to sentencing guidelines relating to certain white-collar offenses

Section 906. Corporate responsibility for financial reports

Title X—Corporate Tax Returns

Title X contains one section that mandates that federal income tax return is to be signed by the CEO.

The Title X section is:

Section 101. Sense of the Senate regarding the signing of corporate tax returns by chief executive officers

Title XI—Corporate Fraud and Accountability

The sections of Title XI provide expanded powers to combat and investigate fraud for the SEC, including payment freezes, as well as increasing penalties for violations of the Securities Exchange Act. This section also takes a preventive approach and prohibits those individuals who have been convicted of fraud-related activities from being executives.

The sections of Title XI are:

Section 1101. Short title

Section 1102. Tampering with a record or otherwise impeding an official proceeding

Section 1103. Temporary freeze authority for the SEC

Section 1104. Amendment to the Federal Sentencing Guidelines

Section 1105. Authority of the Commission to prohibit persons from serving as officers or directors

Section 1106. Increased criminal penalties under Securities Exchange Act of 1934

Section 1107. Retaliation against informants

Glossary

American Depository Receipts (ADRs) Shares of foreign companies that are sold on the U.S. markets through an intermediary, usually a bank.

Auditor An independent assessor who conducts a systematic check or assessment. In the case of SOX, it is an assessment of publicly traded companies' internal controls.

Control Objectives for Informational and Related Technology (COBIT) The most popular internal information technology (IT) control framework for companies seeking SOX compliance.

Code of Ethics A set of rules according to which people in a particular profession are expected to model their behaviors and decisions.

Committee of Sponsoring Organizations (COSO) An internal control framework used in achieving SOX compliance.

Customer Relationship Management (CRM) A software strategy that is adopted by companies that would like to improve efficiency and revenue by fostering customer loyalty.

Enterprise Resource Planning (ERP) Software A platform to integrate all of a company's departments and functions into one dynamic system.

Foreign Issuer International companies that are traded on the U.S. markets.

Generally Accepted Accounting Principles (GAAP) Procedures and standards to guide companies as they assemble their financial statements. The prime objective of these standards is to provide a common reporting system so that investors have a platform for company comparison.

Health Insurance Portability and Accountability Act (HIPAA) An act that requires companies to create systems to protect the privacy and security of documents related to their employees health insurance.

National Institute of Standards and Technology (NIST) A nonregulatory federal agency that was established within the U.S. Commerce Department's Technology Administration in 1901.

Public Company Accounting Oversight Board (PCAOB) An organization created by the Sarbanes-Oxley Act to oversee the auditors of public companies and their activities.

SAS 70 A document that certifies that the service organization has received an in-depth audit of their relevant internal controls.

XBRL Extensible Business Reporting Language, an XML-based standard for defining and exchanging financial information.

Index